CABINS
COTTAGES

Revised & Expanded Edition

Images obtained from Shutterstock.com are by the following photographers: Ann Moore: page 158 bottom right; Anna Nar: back cover middle left, page 29; anthony Heflin: page 163 bottom right; AVN Photo: top borders throughout; B Brown: page 158 bottom left; Cool Vector Maker: Safety Tips symbols throughout; David Fonseca: page 160 bottom left; debra millet: page 159; givaga: page 161; Iris van den Broek: page 157; Jesse Seniunas: page 164 bottom right; JessHarrison: page 164 bottom left; John C. Clarke: page 163 bottom left; jtoddpope: page 163 top; LabDancestrokes: back cover top right, page 9; lastdjedai: page 158 top; ppa: back cover bottom right, page 164 top; Richard Bacon: page 162; shark girl: page 160 top; Silke Stahr: page 160 bottom right; solepsizm: front cover, back cover background, pages 2/3, 4/5; thieury: back cover bottom left; Whiteaster: page 63. From iStockphoto.com: dlewis33: back cover top left; Dorin_S: page 125.

Cabins & Cottages, Revised & Expanded Edition (ISBN 978-1-56523-967-8, 2018) is a revised edition of *Cabins & Cottages* (ISBN 978-1-56523-539-7, 2011), published by Fox Chapel Publishing Company, Inc.

Portions of text and art previously published by and reproduced under license with Direct Holdings Americas Inc.

ISBN 978-1-56523-967-8

Library of Congress Cataloging-in-Publication Data

Names: Fox Chapel Publishing. | Skills Institute Press.
Title: Cabins & cottages.
Other titles: Cabins and cottages
Description: Revised & expanded edition. | Mount Joy, PA : Fox Chapel
  Publishing Company, Inc., [2018] | Includes index. | "Skills Institute Press."
Identifiers: LCCN 2018010519 (print) | LCCN 2018012290 (ebook) | ISBN
  9781607655336 () | ISBN 9781565239678
Subjects: LCSH: Vacation homes--Design and construction--Amateurs' manuals. |
  Log cabins--Design and construction--Amateurs' manuals. | Cottages--Design
  and construction--Amateurs' manuals. | Building--Amateurs' manuals.
Classification: LCC TH4835 (ebook) | LCC TH4835 .C33 2018 (print) | DDC
  690/.837--dc22
LC record available at https://lccn.loc.gov/2018010519

To learn more about the other great books from Fox Chapel Publishing, or to find a retailer near you, call toll-free 800-457-9112 or visit us at *www.FoxChapelPublishing.com*.

We are always looking for talented authors. To submit an idea, please send a brief inquiry to acquisitions@foxchapelpublishing.com.

Printed in China
Second printing

CABINS & COTTAGES

Revised & Expanded Edition

The Basics of Building a Getaway Retreat for Hunting, Camping, and Rustic Living

Distributed By
Fox Chapel Publishing

FOX CHAPEL
PUBLISHING

Table of Contents

What You Can Learn

Making the Most of Your Location, page 8

Choose the safest spot to place your cabin and learn about elements that strengthen or protect it.

Getting Started, page 28

Before you begin building a vacation home, you need to prepare the site.

Four Simple Structures, page 62

Whether you want a sophisticated chalet or a rustic retreat, you can begin with one of these four basic structures.

Adding the Amenities, page 124

Learn to equip your cabin with some of the basic necessities like water, heat, and waste disposal.

Chapter 1

MAKING THE MOST OF YOUR LOCATION

Choosing a location for your vacation home is one of the most important decisions you will make. The features that make some vacation retreats desirable—such as a nearby lake, river, or ocean; or a region covered by deep snow in winter—can also make a location a poor building site. But even in these areas, the following chapter will help you choose the safest spot to place your cabin, and teach you to add elements that strengthen or protect the structure as you build.

Strengthening a House in Earthquake Country

Earthquakes occur in many parts of North America with enough force to shake a building to pieces. If you plan to build a vacation home in any of these areas (map, right), you will need to reinforce the structure.

A Solid Base

Begin with a masonry-block foundation *(page 48)*, but stiffen it with a skeleton of ⅝-inch (16mm) steel reinforcing bars and fill the block cores with concrete grout *(page 14)*. Vertical rebars cast into the footing provide a strong anchor; depending on the height of the wall and on local code, you may also need special masonry units called bond-beam blocks that permit rebar to run horizontally inside the walls and around the corners without interruption. Check codes to determine which courses need bond-beam blocks and horizontal rebar.

Make grade pegs 16 inches (400mm) long. To fashion the vertical supports, bend rebar *(page 51)* at a right angle 6 inches (150mm) from one end and cut it long enough to extend 25 inches (600mm) above the top of the footing. Bend horizontal bars sharply to turn corners. For skirting vents *(page 13)*, order rebar prebent. For mortar strong enough to maintain a good bond during tremors, mix 2½ gallons (9.5 liters) of Portland cement, 1¼ gallons (4.75 liters) of hydrated lime, and 8¾ gallons (33 liters) of sand for each cubic foot (0.3m³) of mortar mix. Buy premixed grout, or blend 1 gallon (3.8 liters) of cement, 2½ gallons (9.5 liters) of sand, 1½ gallons (5.7 liters) of coarse aggregate, and ½ gallon (1.9 liters) of water.

Additional Protection

A strong foundation alone does not provide enough support for a cabin with stud walls. You can brace the walls with plywood sheathing *(page 15)*.

TOOLS

- Maul
- Hammer
- Shovel
- Plumb bob
- Water level
- Rebar cutter
- Square-edged shovel
- Wooden float
- Chalk line
- Mason's trowel
- Mason's level
- Mason's line
- Tin snips
- Brickset
- Ball-peen hammer
- Circular saw

MATERIALS

- 1 x 2s (25 x 50mm), 1 x 6s (25 x 150mm)
- 2 x 4s (50 x 100mm)
- Plywood (⅜" [9mm])
- Exterior plywood siding (⁷⁄₁₆" [12mm])
- Ring-shank nails (2½" [65mm])
- Galvanized box nails (2" [50mm])
- Powdered chalk
- Concrete mix
- Mortar mix
- Rebar (⅝" [16mm]), supports, and safety caps
- Mechanic's wire (16-gauge [1.2mm])
- Polyethylene sheeting
- Concrete blocks
- Bond-beam blocks
- Metal mesh
- Vents
- Grout
- Anchor bolts (½" x 8" [M12 x 200mm]), washers, and nuts

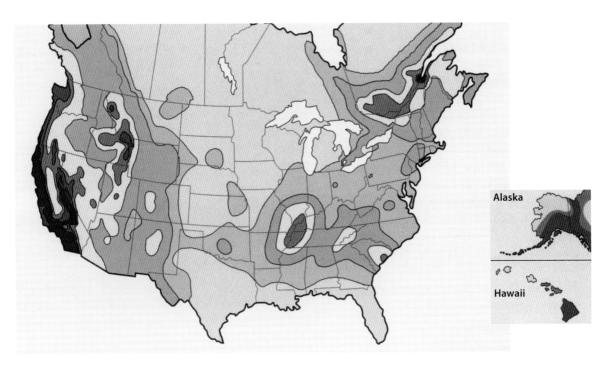

Seismic areas

In this map of North America, dark red sections represent areas where the risk of severe earthquakes is greatest. If you are building in these zones, the special building techniques on the following pages are advisable. In light red areas, major earthquakes are less likely but still possible; consult local building codes to find out whether reinforcement is necessary. Orange, yellow, green, or beige areas represent a decreasing likelihood of seismic activity, and in pink areas, earthquakes are rare and codes usually require no additional reinforcement for new construction.

Wear goggles and a dust mask when mixing mortar. Put on heavy gloves and work boots when working with concrete blocks, and goggles to cut blocks or pour grout.

Bolstering a Foundation Wall

Supporting vertical rebar

Dig the footing trench and lay ⅝-inch (16mm) horizontal reinforcement *(page 52)*.

Rebar Support
Grade Peg
Vertical Re

Tie a string between the batter-boards to mark the center of the planned wall.

Cut two short pieces of rebar for cross ties and lash the ties across the horizontal rebar 16 inches (400mm) apart—or spaced according to building codes. Omit ties where you will lay solid blocks under girder pockets.

With 16-gauge (1.2mm) mechanic's wire, lash prebent vertical rebars to the cross ties as tightly as possible *(right)*.

When all the bars are wired in place, pour the footing *(page 52)*, keeping the vertical rebar straight.

Place a safety cap over each vertical rebar to prevent injury while you are building the wall.

A Quick Mix for Mortar

You can simplify the job of preparing mortar with a rented portable electric mortar mixer *(right)*. This model, with large tires for negotiating rough terrain, is light and easy to move. Shovel the dry ingredients into the drum, then add water gradually until the mix has the desired consistency. Position a container under the chute to catch the mortar when you discharge it from the mixer.

Building the first courses

Spread a 10-inch-wide (250mm) and 1½-inch-thick (40mm) mortar bed on the footing, then start building the foundation at each corner of the footing *(page 53)*, placing the blocks over the vertical rebar.

Level the blocks *(page 53)*.

Lay the subsequent courses in the same way *(right)*, omitting the mesh at every third course as in a standard block-wall foundation, until a bond-beam course is called for. Add vents as necessary *(page 54)*, placing rebar that has been prebent and cut to length to skirt the vents.

Safety Cap

Standard Corner Block

Making bond-beam corner blocks

Adapt a standard corner block to allow horizontal rebar to turn each corner in a bond-beam course: With a brickset and ball-peen hammer, chisel the middle web and the webs that will abut blocks at the corner *(left)* to the level of the webs in a bond-beam block.

Making a bond beam

With tin snips, cut pieces of metal mesh to fit over one core of each standard block.

Embed the mesh in mortar over every block core without vertical rebar, then lay a course of bond-beam blocks *(right, inset)* as for standard blocks, placing the modified corner blocks at each corner and solid blocks for girder pockets as for a standard wall.

Remove the safety caps from the ends of the vertical rebars.

On the webs of the bond-beam blocks around the entire course, set two rebars parallel to each other and 2 inches (50mm) apart. Bend the rebars to turn the corners and overlap 12 inches (300mm) at each end. Cut the rebars at the solid blocks below the girder pockets.

With 16-gauge (1.2mm) mechanic's wire, fasten the overlapped ends together *(right)*.

If the bond-beam course is the top course in the wall, grout it. If it is an intermediate course, wire a second length of vertical rebar to the end of each existing piece of vertical rebar, overlapping the bars 30 inches (750mm) and with the second piece extending 16 inches (400mm). Cover each one with a safety cap, and continue adding courses of standard block.

Grouting the wall

Before mixing and pouring grout, prepare to embed anchor bolts for the sill plate in the grout *(page 55)*. If you plan to brace the cabin against wind with anchor-downs, make the bolts at door and window openings long enough to pass through the soleplates of the stud walls *(page 17)*. Pour grout into all the cores containing vertical rebar and into the bond-beam blocks. Have a helper follow to compact the grout with a stick to remove air pockets *(above)*. (The mesh placed over the cores without rebar will keep the grout from filling those cores.)

With a mason's trowel, strike off the grout flush with the tops of the bond-beam blocks.

Stiffening the Frame

Adding sheathing

Assemble and put up walls in the same way you would for prefabricated walls *(page 64)*, but instead of nailing on only siding, first fasten ⅜-inch (9mm) plywood sheathing. Space the panels ⅛ inch (3mm) apart and nail them to the studs, top plate, and soleplate every 6 inches (150mm) around the perimeter, and every 12 inches (300mm) in between, with 2-inch (50mm) box nails. If your cabin is in an area subject to earthquakes or hurricanes, check local codes; the sheathing may need to be thicker and the nails spaced closer together—from 2 to 4 inches (50-100mm) apart. Fasten ⁷⁄₁₆-inch (12mm) exterior siding to the sheathing with 2½-inch (65mm) galvanized nails driven at 6-inch (150mm) intervals around the perimeter and at 12-inch (300mm) intervals along the intermediate studs, spacing the panels ⅛ inch (3mm) apart and offsetting their edges from those of the sheathing panels by 16 inches (400mm).

A Trio of Earthquake Valves

Three valves

Designed for professional installation, earthquake valves come in a wide range of designs and prices. Simplest and least expensive is the valve at left, which consists of a metal ball perched on a ramp. When the valve is jolted by a tremor, the ball rolls off the ramp and over the gas line, stopping the flow of gas. In the more sensitive valve at center, a metal ball triggers a latch mechanism that clamps against the outlet end of the valve like a closing door. Most sophisticated is the valve at right, which bears the seal of approval of Underwriters Laboratories, the fire-protection organization whose recommendation is most widely accepted by fire-fighting agencies and insurance companies. In this valve, a pendulum-weighted lower pin supports an upper pin set into a disk. When an earthquake strikes, the pendulum holds the lower pin stationary; the upper pin, dislodged by the tremor, falls downward and the disk plugs the valve seat.

Tying a House Together Against Wind

Violent winds can easily destroy a vacation home, literally ripping off the roof or tearing the walls loose from their foundation. If your cabin is in an area subject to hurricanes, such as the Atlantic and Gulf coasts, you can take steps to anchor the structure. Check local building codes to see if reinforcement of your cabin is required.

Reinforcing the Structure
For a cabin built with stud walls, use special hardware to anchor the studs and soleplates to the foundation, the band and header joists to the sill plates, the walls to the band and header joists, and the roof rafters to the studs. If you plan to take such measures, build a block-wall foundation *(page 53)*, embedding bolts for the anchor-downs that will adjoin door and window openings *(opposite)* long enough to pass through the subfloor and soleplates. Frame the walls as for a prefab cottage *(page 64)*, but drill holes through the soleplates for the anchor bolts, and raise the walls and install the hardware before nailing the siding. Until the siding is in place, support the walls with diagonal bracing attached to stakes driven into the ground *(page 97)*. Consult local codes or a building professional for the type and placement of hardware needed.

Additional Precautions
When a storm threatens, you can weight down the roof of your cabin with sandbags for extra protection. Also board up windows, leaving one or two slightly open on the lee—or sheltered—side of the house to equalize the air pressure inside and out. During a hurricane the higher air pressure indoors can burst doors and windows out of their frames.

TOOLS
- Socket wrench
- Hammer
- Keyhole saw

MATERIALS
- Anchor-downs and lag screws
- Connector plates and nails
- Strap ties and nails
- Hurricane ties and nails
- Silicone caulk
- Rafter-to-stud connectors and nails
- Wall-covering repair materials

Safety Tips

Goggles protect your eyes when you are hammering.

Reinforcing a Cabin

Anchoring the walls

On each side of door and window openings, use a socket wrench to fasten the horizontal flange of an anchor-down to the anchor bolt in the foundation. Bolt the vertical flange to the outside of the king stud with the lag screws recommended by the manufacturer *(above, left)*.

At every second stud, tie the band or header joist to the sill plate with a connector plate, fastened with the nails recommended by the manufacturer, then fasten a strap tie across the seam between each stud and the band or header joist with the recommended nails, filling all the holes in the strap *(above, right)*.

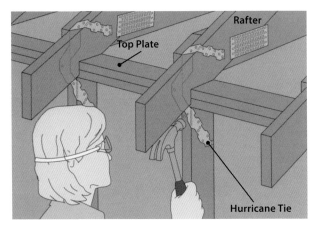

Strapping the roof to the wall

With the nails recommended by the anchor manufacturer, nail one flange of a hurricane tie to a rafter and the other to the top plate of the wall *(left)*.

Repeat the procedure to install an anchor at every rafter.

Measures for Existing Structures

Anchoring floors and walls

At every second stud, align a strap tie vertically on the wall siding over the sill plate, band or header joist, soleplate, and stud.

With the nails recommended by the manufacturer, fasten the tie to the wall, driving a nail into each hole in the strap *(right)*.

If the siding is uneven or angled, as with clapboard or vinyl siding, cut through it with a keyhole saw to make a recess for the strap, then nail the strap directly to the sheathing. Seal the cut with silicone caulking.

Linking walls and roof

Inside the cabin, remove sections of the wall covering with a keyhole saw to expose every second joint between the studs, top plate, and rafters.

Nail one flange of a rafter-to-stud connector to the rafter and the other to the stud with the manufacturer's recommended nails *(left)*.

Repair the wall covering.

The Lay of the Land: Clues to Foil a Flood

Water can be a threat to a country cabin. Rushing in a torrent, trickling down a slope, or rising from a flooded river, it can damage or destroy the sturdiest structure. To some extent you can meet the danger by using a special method of construction—building a cabin on a set of high poles, for example *(page 37)*, may raise the structure above flood levels—but the real key to protecting a cabin from floods is the right choice of a building site.

Avoiding Troublespots

Sometimes the choice of site is fairly obvious. The closer a cabin is to a river or lake, the more likely it is to be damaged in a flood. Elsewhere, the problems of correct siting are relatively subtle, and locations that seem ideal at first glance may turn out to be the most vulnerable. A site next to a peaceful stream at the bottom of a ravine or valley, for example, may look safe, especially if you set your cabin well above the water level. Actually, it is a site to be avoided. During or after a heavy rain, the stream is likely to rise rapidly and flow with great force, destroying any property in its path. Other danger spots, along with the safest locations to build on them, are shown on pages 20 and 21.

Assessing a Site

A surveyor or landscape architect can identify potential flood problems for you, but you can do a good deal of preliminary detective work yourself. Start by asking neighbors and the area office of the Soil Conservation Service about the history of flooding at or near the site you are considering. Then study the site itself during a rainstorm. As the water runs off, you will see it flowing or collecting in natural drainage paths—areas that should not be blocked by any structure you build.

Vegetation and topographic features give additional clues to potential problems. Plants growing in a generally arid plot of ground indicate a spot that may become a short-lived pond or waterway during a heavy rain. Smooth, rounded boulders were probably shaped by water flowing over them repeatedly in the past. Level ground near creeks and streams is a likely sign of periodic flooding.

A steep ravine or valley

The cabin in the background is sited much too close to a
stream running along the bottom of a narrow ravine. In a
storm, the volume and velocity of the stream will increase,
and water will rise up the sides of the steep slope. The
cabin in the forefront, situated on a gradual slope well
away from the stream, is safe from such flash floods.

An upland meadow

The cabin in the center of the picture is located in a depressed area that collects rainwater, and the driveway that links it to a main road cuts across the natural drainage path around the building site; in a storm, this roadway would channel water directly into the dishlike meadow. The cabin to the right is built on a higher site that drains quickly; its driveway follows the contour of the land, and underground culverts protect the driveway from a washout.

Culverts

Near a river

The cabin in the foreground is built in the oxbow of a river, at the heart of a floodplain; in a heavy rain, the river might widen, completely submerging the site. The cabin in the distance, on a gentle slope well above the flood plain, lies clear of the probable flood pattern.

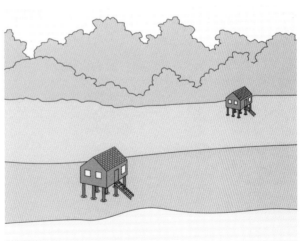

By a lake

On lakefront property, it may be tempting to build a cabin or cottage with the closest and best possible view of the water. But sand is a highly unstable surface on which to build anything of substance. The cabin close to the lake shoreline is vulnerable to high winds and shifting sands. The cabin on the right is positioned safely on slightly elevated and solid ground.

Preparing for Deep Snow

Before constructing a cabin in snow country, you must be sure that you will be able to reach it through deep snow and that the structure will remain comfortable throughout a long, severe winter. Improve access to the cabin by building a raised boardwalk *(page 24)*; its sections can be separated and stored in the spring, then reassembled before the snow falls.

Locating the Cabin

Hilltops tend to be too windy for winter comfort; idyllic-looking "sheltered valleys" are generally reservoirs of deep snow and cold air. The best location for a cabin is on a south-facing slope, which gets light and warmth from the low winter sun. Do not place a building far from a plowed road unless you plan to get to it by snowshoe or with a snowmobile.

Cold-Climate Construction:

Continuous masonry-block foundation walls *(page 53)* are the warmest, and you can insulate them from the outside with packed snow; make sure the base of the foundation rests below the frost line. Insulate walls and install double-glazed glass for windows. Add to comfort and save on fuel costs by shielding the area outside the main door of the cabin with an enclosed entryway *(page 25)*.

The roof of a snow-country cabin may need thick rafters and special bracing to support the snow, or a steep pitch to shed snow *(page 23)*. A roof steep enough to shed snow has an obvious advantage, but it has disadvantages, too. It requires far more roofing material to cover a given floor area, and much of the high space underneath the rafters may be wasted. The rafters of a steep roof must be fastened securely to the wall *(page 92)* to combat strong winds that would flow over a lower roof.

TOOLS

- Circular saw
- Electric drill
- Socket wrench
- Carpenter's level
- Carpenter's square
- Plumb bob
- Auger
- Maul
- Water level
- Hacksaw
- Mason's line
- Handsaw

MATERIALS

- 1 x 2s (25 x 50mm),
  1 x 4s (25 x 100mm),
  1 x 6s (25 x 150mm)
- 2 x 4s (50 x 100mm),
  2 x 6s (50 x 150mm)
- Pressure-treated
  2 x 8s (50 x 200mm),
  2 x 10s (50 x 250mm)
- Exterior grade
  plywood (¾" [18mm])
- Galvanized common nails
  (2" [50mm], 3" [75mm],
  3½" [100mm])

- Ring-shank
  nails (2½" [65mm])
- Lag screws (½" x 6" [M12
  x 150mm])
- Carriage bolts (⅜ x 5" [M10
  x 125mm], 6" [150mm])
- Materials for concrete piers

- Polyethylene sheeting
  (6-mil [heavy-duty])
- Joist hangers, multipurpose
  framing anchors, and nails
- Concrete mix
- Prefabricated stairs
- Siding and roofing materials

Safety Tips

Wear safety goggles when hammering and when operating a power tool. Put on gloves to handle pressure-treated lumber; add a dust mask when cutting it.

A cabin ready for winter's worst

Evergreen trees behind and beside the cabin at right act as windbreaks, but none are close enough to topple onto the roof. Trees have been cleared from the downwind, south side of the cabin to allow the sun to warm it; one deciduous tree remains, blocking little sun in winter but offering shade in summer. Similarly, the cabin's overhanging eaves block the rays of a high, hot summer sun but let in those of a low winter sun. The eaves are extended at one point to shelter an enclosed entryway and the steps leading up to it. A raised board-walk, which can be dismantled in spring, leads from the front steps to the deck and on out to the driveway. A snow fence prevents blowing snow from drifting onto the cabin's driveway in the foreground.

Picking the right size rafters

The chart above lists the correct lumber sizes for rafters spaced 16 inches (400mm) apart on a roof in a snowy region. To use the chart, find the vertical columns for your roof slope, then read down the column to the horizontal row for the rafter span and the snow load in your area. If the exact slope, span, and load for your cabin do not appear on the chart, use the next lower figure for slope, and the next higher for span and load. To get the figure for ground-snow load in your area, check with the local office of the Federal Housing Administration or an architect or structural engineer.

Rafters for Snow Country

Roof Slope	4" in 12" (100mm in 300mm)			7" in 12" (180mm in 300mm)			10" in 12" (250mm in 300mm)			14" in 12" (360mm in 300mm)		
Rafter Span	9' (2.7m)	12' (3.7m)	15' (4.6m)	9' (2.7m)	12' (3.7m)	15' (4.6m)	9' (2.7m)	12' (3.7m)	15' (4.6m)	9' (2.7m)	12' (3.7m)	15' (4.6m)
Snow Load 50 lbs. (23kg)	2 x 6	2 x 8	2 x 10	2 x 6	2 x 8	2 x 10	2 x 6	2 x 8	2 x 10	2 x 6	2 x 8	2 x 8
60 lbs. (27kg)	2 x 6	2 x 10	2 x 10	2 x 6	2 x 8	2 x 10	2 x 6	2 x 8	2 x 10	2 x 6	2 x 8	2 x 8
70 lbs. (32kg)	2 x 8	2 x 10	2 x 12	2 x 6	2 x 10	2 x 10	2 x 6	2 x 8	2 x 10	2 x 6	2 x 8	2 x 10

Rafter Dim. Conversion

2 x 6	50 x 150mm
2 x 8	50 x 200mm
2 x 10	50 x 250mm
2 x 12	50 x 300mm

A roof for heavy snow

The slope of the roof shown at right rises a steep 30 degrees, or 7 inches (180mm) for every 12 inches (300mm) of horizontal run, and is a prudent choice for snow country. If covered with metal roofing *(page 98)*, it will shed snow quickly. A roof of the same slope, covered with asphalt shingles, won't shed snow as well, and to keep melting snow from leaking through, would need flashing extending 8 to 10 inches (200–250mm) above the line of the walls and lapped under the two lowest courses of shingles *(right)*. Clear the roof after heavy snowfalls with a roof rake—a long-handled scraper available from hardware stores or homemade by nailing and bracing a 2-foot (600mm) 1-by-6 (25 x 150mm batten) to the end of a long pole.

A path over snow and mud

The sections of this raised boardwalk can be separated and stored in spring, then reassembled before the first heavy snow. For the walkway, make open boxes of 2-by-6s (50 x 150mm), 6 feet (2m) long and 3 feet (1m) wide, with the long boards nailed to the ends of the shorter ones. Plank the tops of the boxes with 1-by-6s (25 x 150mm) spaced ¼ inch (5mm) apart. For each H-shaped support, use 6-foot (1.8m) 2-by-4 (50mm x 100mm) uprights 3 feet (1m) apart, and bolt a pair of 2-by-4 (50mm x 100mm) crosspieces between them 2 ½ feet (750mm) from the bottom. Nail 1-by-4 (25mm x 100mm) diagonal braces across the bottom half of the H. To assemble the sections, bolt the boxes together between the uprights, resting their bottoms on the crosspieces. Add handrails and 1-by-4 (25mm x 100mm) braces from one H to the next. Attach the end of the boardwalk to the cabin's entryway, and install a flight of steps at the other end.

A Doorway Sheltered from Wind and Snow

Extending the rafters

Miter one end of a 2-by-6 (50 x 150mm) to an angle matching that of the roof slope.

Starting at one side of the planned entryway, set the board alongside one of the main roof rafters with its mitered end up against the house wall and its top aligned with the top of the rafter.

With a carpenter's level, draw a vertical line on the 2-by-6 (50 x 150mm) at the point where you plan to build the outside wall of the entryway *(right)*.

Take the 2-by-6 (50 x 150mm) down and draw a 3½-inch (90mm) line with a carpenter's square at a right angle from the first line to the bottom edge of the 2-by-6 (50 x 150mm) *(inset)*.

Cut the board at the lines with a circular saw and use it as a template to cut a 2-by-6 (50 x 150mm) for each rafter that will extend over the entryway.

At each end of the entryway, nail one of the boards onto a rafter with 3-inch (75mm) galvanized common nails, driving two at both ends, then every 16 inches (400mm) in between in a zigzag pattern.

Bracing the extended rafters

Cut and position 1-by-2 (25 x 50mm) horizontal struts on the house wall to brace the rafter extensions temporarily; if necessary, place shims between the ends of the struts and the wall to align the extensions perfectly with the existing rafters *(left)*.

Hang a plumb bob from the end of one of the extensions to mark the outside edge of a foundation pier for the entryway. Mark the location of a second pier at the opposite end of the entryway; if the distance between the piers is greater than 10 feet (3m), add a third pier in between.

Cast footings for the piers at the same depth as the footings of the cabin and install two masonry piers *(page 43)*.

Assemble a girder from three pressure-treated 2-by-10s (50 x 250mm) and install it atop the piers *(page 46)*, aligning its ends flush with those of the piers.

Shim

Strut

Building the platform support

Make a plate to support the platform's joists at the doorway from a pressure-treated 2-by-8 (50 x 200mm) cut a few inches longer than the desired length of the entryway platform.

At the end of the joist plate opposite the proposed stairs, make a mark 1 inch (25mm) from the end for the first joist; then, continue marking the plate at 16-inch (400mm) intervals for the rest of the joists.

Tack a plumb bob to the outside face of the rafter extension where it meets the wall, and align the joist plate so the outside of the first joist mark is under the plumb bob and the plate's bottom edge is level with the top of the entry-way girder. Have a helper mark it.

Make marks above the joist plate on both sides of the door molding at a height that equals the thickness of the platform's decking, and cut off the bottom of the door molding at these marks.

Fasten the joist plate to the wall with ½-by-6-inch (M12 x 150mm) lag screws.

Move the plumb bob to the end of the rafter extension; then, using a carpenter's square, transfer the joist locations to the girder *(right)*.

Joist Plate

First Joist Mark

Girder

Hanging the joists

At the marks on the joist plate, nail joist hangers.

Place pressure-treated 2-by-8 (50 x 200mm) joists in the hangers, and set their ends on the girder marks.

Nail the joist hangers to the joists *(left)*. Attach the other end of the joists to the girder with multipurpose framing anchors.

Add a platform of ¾-inch (18mm) exterior-grade plywood, fastening it to the joists with 2½-inch (65mm) ring-shank nails *(page 59)*; or nail decking of pressure-treated 2-by-6s (50 x 150mm), separated by ¼ inch (5mm).

Pour shallow concrete footings and fasten a set of prefabricated steps to the end joist with framing anchors *(page 84)*.

Top Plate

Soleplate

Framing the outside wall

Cut two 2-by-4s (50 x 100mm) to the length of the outside wall for a top and sole-plate and mark them for studs to align with the rafter extensions.

Because the soleplate will rest on both the entryway floor and on the girder, the studs will be of unequal lengths: Cut the plate to the length of the floor and cut studs to fit between the top plate and the two sections of soleplate when the wall is fastened to the rafter extensions.

Attach the studs to the top plate and the soleplate sections with 3½-inch (100mm) common nails *(above)*.

With a helper, lift the frame into position. Nail the soleplate to the girder and toenail it through the entryway floor into the joists.

Toenail the rafter extensions to the top plate, then remove the struts.

Install the remaining rafter extensions and toenail them to the top plate.

Framing the end walls

Cut a soleplate for the end wall of the entryway and nail it to the floor.

Hold a stud against the end rafter extension and mark it to create a 1½-inch-deep (40mm) notch *(right and inset)*.

Mark other studs in the same way 16 inches (400mm) apart to complete the wall.

Cut the studs at the marks and attach each one to the rafter with two 3-inch (75mm) galvanized common nails.

Install siding over the stud walls and extend the roofing, slipping the new roofing under the existing layer.

Platform

Notch

End Soleplate

Footing

Chapter 2
GETTING STARTED

Before you can begin building a vacation home, you will need to prepare the site. In the absence of heavy machinery such as bulldozers or tractors, tools like chain saws and come-alongs can substantially lighten the work of felling trees and removing logs and boulders. When the area is cleared, you can begin construction by laying a foundation that suits the site and type of structure you plan to build.

Generating Power

Electricity is indispensable during the construction of a vacation home, either to power electric tools or to recharge the batteries of cordless models. If the building site is close to power lines, you can have the utility company install a temporary power drop; if it lies miles from electric lines, a portable generator can produce electricity on the spot, and can become a permanent feature once the structure is built.

Portable Generators

The smallest practical unit for powering portable tools has a generating capacity of 2,000 watts, enough to run a 7¼-inch (185mm) circular saw. If you plan to use stationary tools, you'll need one that can produce about 3,500 watts. When your building plans include a well with an electric pump

(page 132), obtain a unit that generates 4,000 watts or more, and install it in a permanent, sheltered location. Consider a model that can be switched from 120 to 240 volts to supply the current necessary to run a submersible pump. A unit that supplies up to 7,000 watts can operate additional electric devices such as lights or a refrigerator.

A Temporary Power Drop

Consisting of an electric meter, a weatherproof service panel, and weatherproof receptacles, a power drop mounts on a pole or at any location convenient to the site. Choose a location that will be out of the way during construction, but one that is close enough that you do not need to string extension cords together or extend wires to reach the building. When the time comes, it will be simple to move the meter and panel or extend wires from the power drop to the cabin or cottage.

Muffler   Gas Tank   Ignition Switch   Outlet Switch   Outlet Box   Alternator   Frame   Engine

A portable power plant

A typical generator consists of a gas-powered engine that drives an alternator to produce the standard alternating current. The power is made available through receptacles in an outlet box; an outlet switch turns power to the receptacles on and off. The components are attached to a frame fitted with carrying handles. The engine requires about the same maintenance as that of a lawn mower—periodic replenishment and replacement of oil, and an occasional new spark plug.

Clearing the Building Site

Once you have chosen an appropriate site for your vacation retreat, you'll need to remove underbrush, trees, and boulders from the area. This can be a formidable task, but it is mostly a matter of picking the right tool for each job and using it simply and safely.

Clearing Vegetation

Cut bushes down to ground level with a pair of pruning shears, and dig the roots up with a shovel the same way you would those of a small tree *(page 36)*. Clear tall grass and vines with a gas-powered trimmer; or use a scythe or a hand sickle, always holding your free hand away from the blade.

Removing Trees

Felling large, mature trees is a complex and dangerous operation that is best left to professional loggers. One big risk is that the vibration of sawing dislodges a dead branch high overhead, which then falls onto the sawyer. Another is causing the tree to fall in an unwanted direction, onto your vehicle for example. A third risk is that the falling tree becomes entangled with adjacent trees, a situation that requires both experience and specialized equipment to resolve.

A lightweight chain saw with a 14-inch (35cm) or 16-inch (40cm) bar gives you the capacity to fell and buck small trees up to about 8 inches (200mm) in diameter. Before you start cutting, however, you must take the time to study the location and lean of the tree, and plan where you intend it to fall. It is easy to fall a tree in the direction of its natural lean, and it's possible, with good planning and sawing technique, and careful use of wedges, to direct the fall away from the natural lean *(page 32)*.

Removing Rocks

For stones that are too large for you to budge, wrap rope or a chain around them and use a come-along *(page 35)*. Or, split them into smaller pieces that can be moved more easily: Fit a drill with a masonry bit and bore holes in the rocks, then drive in steel wedges with a sledgehammer.

Caution

Before you start cutting any tree, plan an escape route—ideally at about a 45-degree angle from the proposed direction of the fall—and remove all obstacles from the path. Carefully study the tree's crown for dead and partially broken branches, and see if you can dislodge them before you begin to saw. If not, consider the risk of the dead branch falling on your head, and consider calling in professional help.

TOOLS
- Chain saw
- Sledgehammer
- Wooden wedges

The Safe Way to Fell a Tree

Cutting a notch in the trunk

On the side of the tree that faces the direction of its natural lean, hold a chain saw with the blade angled at 45 degrees to the trunk.

Turn on the engine, let it come to full throttle, and make an angled cut about one-third of the way through the trunk. Pull the blade from the cut.

Holding the blade horizontally at the bottom of the angled cut, saw to the end of the cut *(right)*. Retract the blade and push the wedge-shaped piece from the notch.

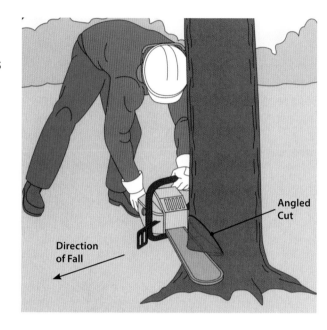

Angled
Cut

Direction
of Fall

A Lightweight Chain Saw

In addition to severing small tree trunks and branches, a lightweight chain saw can double as an all-purpose wood-cutting tool. Although not as powerful as a heavy-duty model, and therefore unable to cut larger trunks, a lightweight saw can be handled by the average person, whereas a heavy saw is liable to be unwieldy, awkward, and very tiring to use.

Making the felling cut

On the side of the trunk opposite the notch, start a horizontal cut 2 inches (50mm) above the bottom of the notch *(right)*.

Stop cutting when the blade is 2 to 3 inches from the back of the notch, creating a hinge *(inset)*. The trunk will pivot on the hinge, and the tree should fall. If not, drive in wedges *(page 34)*.

Felling Cut

Notch

Hinge

Notch

Chain Saw Safety Gear

If you are clearing away a large number of trees with a chain saw, it is essential to wear special safety clothing. Leg coverings, or chaps, as well as the boots and gloves, are lined with a protective material such as Kevlar that is reinforced to resist being cut through. The helmet incorporates ear protection and a face shield.

Cut-resistant Gloves

Helmet with Ear Muffs and Face Shield

Safety Boots

Protective Chaps

Felling Trees in Difficult Situations

Felling a sharply leaning tree

As shown in the inset, a series of cuts is necessary to fell a tree that leans sharply. First, make shallow cuts on each side of the trunk parallel to the direction of fall *(right)* to prevent the tree from splitting behind the notch cut.

At the same level as the side cuts—but perpendicular to them—cut a notch halfway into the trunk *(page 32)*.

Finally, make the felling cut *(page 33)*.

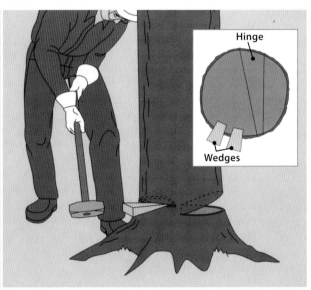

Felling away from the lean

Cut a notch on the side of the tree facing the direction that you want the tree to fall *(page 32)*.

For the felling cut *(page 33)*, angle the chain saw blade so the hinge will be thicker opposite the natural direction of the lean, then make the cut *(above, left)*.

Drive wooden or plastic wedges into the felling cut near the thin side of the hinge *(above, right)*; the wedges will force the tree upward on that side, shifting its center of gravity away from the lean. If driving in the wedges does not cause the tree to fall, drive in thicker wedges.

Removing Logs, Stumps, and Roots

Once large trees are cut down, you can maneuver the logs around your building site with a hand-operated come-along. Rather than chopping down small trees and then getting rid of the roots, you can uproot them *(page 36)*, then dispose of them.

Transplanting Trees

If you opt for transplanting, keep in mind that trees taller than 10 feet (3m) with trunks that are greater than 3 inches (75mm) thick will be unwieldy to move and will be less likely to survive when replanted. A tree's chances are greatest if you transplant in a period of low growth activity—in spring, or autumn.

Moving Logs

The come-along, a tool with a ratchet mechanism and a lever that is moved back and forth to reel in a cable, gives you the mechanical advantage needed to clear out heavy logs by hand *(below)*.

Removing Stumps

For trees that were already cut down, uproot small stumps the same way you would a small tree; larger ones can be ground down to below grade using a rented stump cutter *(page 36)*. For very large stumps, it's best to hire a professional to remove them.

Protective Sleeve

Come-along

Cable

Dragging a log with a come-along

Wrap a heavy-duty chain with a hook around the log, about 2 feet (600mm) from the end, using the hook to hold the chain in place.

Fasten a second chain, without a hook, around the trunk of a tree in the direction you want to pull the log.

Unless you will be cutting down this tree, protect the bark with a sleeve, such as a bicycle inner tube.

Hook the extendable cable of a come-along *(inset)* to the chain on the log, and hook the stationary end to the chain around the tree. Draw the log toward the tree by moving the handle on the come-along back and forth *(above)*.

Safety Tips

Wear steel-toed safety boots when moving logs.

TOOLS
- Heavy-duty chains
- Hook for chain
- Come-along
- Flate spade

Digging Out Small Trees or Stumps

Removing the rootball

Using a flat spade with a sharp blade, slice through the roots in a 30- to 36-inch-wide (75–100cm) circle around the trunk. Push the blade into the ground at about a 30-degree angle toward the trunk to taper the root ball for easy removal *(right)*.

Dig a 24- to 30-inch-deep (60–75cm) access trench around the rootball.

Sever the taproot—the root section that heads straight down into the ground—and any other uncut roots under the tree with the spade. With a helper, lift out the tree and rootball.

Taproot

Rootball

A Portable Stump Cutter

An alternative to the labor-intensive process of chopping or digging up stumps is to rent a stump cutter. This gas-powered machine has an angled blade that shaves a stump down to ground level quickly and easily. On some models, the handlebars can be attached to a holder at one end of the tool, as shown here, or to a longer holder at the other end, to allow the cutter to reach stumps near obstructions. A tough rubber flap deflects chips away from the operator, but be sure to wear goggles when you are running the machine.

A Foundation on Poles

From a distance, a cottage resting on wooden poles may look shaky and fragile. In reality, such a foundation can provide decades of stalwart support and withstand storms and floods.

Site Suitability

Pole platforms cannot be used everywhere. In some localities, building codes require continuous-wall foundations. Walls are also recommended in earthquake-prone regions, cold climates, and on building sites with insecure soil—such as sand or soft clay—or a slope greater than 1 in 10—1 foot of rise for every 10 horizontal feet (1m for every 10m). The techniques on these pages are designed only for fairly level sites with stable soil.

Lumber and Concrete

Buy pressure-treated poles that are reasonably straight and uniform in diameter, and get enough to space them about 8 feet (2.4m) apart. For a level site, they need to be long enough to extend 1½ to 3 feet (0.5–1m) above ground level and at least 4 feet (1.2m) below it, or at least 6 inches (150mm) below the frost line if it is deeper than 4 feet (1.2m). Where the ground slopes gently, buy poles that are 1 foot longer (300mm). For the beams, obtain pressure-treated lumber long enough to span the rows of poles.

To anchor poles in their holes, you will need concrete or a wet mixture of 1 part Portland cement to 5 parts clean soil, free of roots, leaves, and other organic matter. Prepare this mixture by combining the dry ingredients, then adding slightly less water than you would for concrete—the amount of water will vary depending on the soil.

TOOLS

- Maul
- Hammer
- Tape measure (50-foot [30m])
- Plumb bob
- Power auger
- Garden spade
- Posthole digger
- Carpenter's level
- Line level
- 2 x 4 (50 x 100mm) tamper
- Bucksaw
- Electric drill with auger bit (½" [12mm])
- Wrench
- Circular saw

MATERIALS

- 1 x 2s (25 x 50mm), 1 x 6s (25 x 150mm)
- 2 x 4s (50 x 100mm), 2 x 8s (50 x 200mm)
- Pressure-treated poles (6"–8" thick [150–200mm])
- Pressure-treated 2 x 6s (50 x 150mm), 2 x 10s (50 x 250mm)
- Exterior-grade plywood (¾" [18mm])
- Ring-shank nails (2" [50mm])
- Galvanized common nails (2½" [65mm], 3" [75mm])
- Multipurpose framing anchors and nails
- Carriage bolts (½" [M12]), washers, and nuts
- Powdered chalk
- Concrete mix or Portland cement and clean soil

Safety Tips

Goggles protect your eyes when you are using power tools or hammering. Wear gloves when handling pressure-treated wood; add a dust mark when cutting it.

Plywood

Header Joist

Middle Beams

Joist

Corner Pole

Middle Pole

Inside Beam

Framing Anchor

Intermediate Pole

Outside Beam

Corner Pole

Anatomy of a pole platform

A foundation 16 feet square (4.8m²) consists of three rows of pressure-treated poles sunk into the ground at 8-foot (2.4m) intervals. Each pole is firmly anchored in a jacket of concrete or soil-cement mixture; the tops of the poles are sandwiched between 2-by-10 (50 x 250mm) pressure-treated beams, fastened in place with ½-inch (M12) carriage bolts, washers, and nuts. The 2-by-6 (50 x 150mm) pressure-treated floor joists, which span from the outside beams to the middle beams, are fastened to the beams with framing anchors. They are also nailed to a header joist at each end of the foundation. The outer joists are placed to coincide with the eventual location of the cabin's walls. Sheets of plywood nailed across the joists can serve as a subfloor or as a finish floor.

Putting up a Pole Platform

Digging the holes

Lay out the site as you would for a block wall *(page 48)*, marking the location of the poles in relation to the walls.

Rent a power auger to dig each posthole to a depth of 4 feet (1.2m) or at least 6 inches (150mm) below the frost line, whichever is deeper. You can use a one-man power auger *(inset)*, but a two-man version *(right)* is more powerful and easier to handle.

With a spade and a clamshell posthole digger, widen the holes to 16 to 18 inches (400–450mm) in diameter.

Set all the poles in their holes.

On a gently sloping site—one with a rise of 1 in 10 or less—you will need to dig the postholes deeper and larger than those on a level site; consult local building codes or a building professional.

Pole Location

Setting the poles

Plumb the corner poles with a level and, while a helper holds them straight, brace them with 1-by-2s (25 x 50mm) nailed to stakes.

Measure down from the top of one corner pole the width of a beam plus 3 inches (75mm), and make a mark there. Drive a nail at the mark.

Stretch a string fitted with a line level from the nail to the other corner post, and mark the second corner post at the height of the level string. Drive a nail there and tie the string to it.

Align the middle pole with the string, then plumb and brace it. Mark the point where the string touches the pole.

Prepare enough concrete or cement-soil mixture to fill in around the poles and shovel it into each hole, overfilling it slightly. Tamp the mixture with a 2-by-4 (50 x 100mm), sloping the top downward from the pole to the ground.

Repeat the process on the other rows of poles, then remove the strings and nails and let the concrete cure for a day.

Starting the daps

To enable the beams to sit squarely against the poles, you'll need to cut a notch, called a dap, on both sides of each pole near the top. With a bucksaw or pruning saw, first make a series of horizontal cuts 1½ inches (40mm) wide and ⅛ to ¼ inch (3–6mm) deep on one side of the pole *(right)*. Work from the top of the pole to the beam mark.

Beam Mark

Dap

Finishing the daps

Place the saw on top of the pole and align the blade with the ends of the horizontal cuts on one side, then saw down through the cuts from the top of the pole to the beam mark *(left)*.

Cut daps on the same side of the remaining poles.

Working with Concrete in the Wilderness

To save you the trouble of having to mix separate ingredients for concrete—Portland cement, sand, and gravel—get the cement and sand premixed. Since the site is unlikely to have shelter during the early stages of construction, protect the dry ingredients by placing the bags on wooden pallets and covering them with plastic sheets or tarpaulins. To clean up your tools after a day's work without the luxury of running water, keep a 6-gallon (30-liter) bucket of water on hand, and when you're finished with a tool, place it in the bucket. Replace the water as necessary, but use it to clean out the wheelbarrow before discarding it.

Locating the outside beams

With a helper, set a beam against the outside of one row of poles so the bottom edge sits squarely in the daps in the posts.

Holding the beam level, temporarily fasten it to each pole with a 3-inch (75mm) common nail *(left)*.

Nail a beam to the outsides of each remaining row of poles in the same way.

Cut the tops of the poles flush with the tops of the beams.

Positioning the inside beams

With a helper, run a string across a row of poles on the side opposite the beam *(above)*.

Line up the string with the edge of the pole that is smallest in diameter *(inset)*.

Mark the tops of the larger poles at the string line, and cut a dap at each mark.

Temporarily nail beams to the inside of the poles as described above.

Bolting the beams to the poles

Measure and mark a point one-third of the way from the top and bottom of each beam.

Install a ½-inch (12mm) auger bit in an electric drill and bore a hole through the beams and pole at each mark *(above)*.

Insert a ½-inch (M12) carriage bolt about 1 inch (25mm) longer than the combined thickness of the beams and pole into each hole.

Tighten washers and nuts onto the bolts.

As wood tends to shrink over time, check the nuts for tightness several weeks after the foundation is completed, and tighten them as necessary.

Attaching the floor joists

Set the joists across the beams at 16-inch (400mm) intervals, letting them extend beyond the outside beams by a foot (300mm) and overlap at the center beams by a foot (300mm).

With 3-inch (75mm) common nails, fasten together the joists that overlap at the center beams.

Fasten the joists to the beams with multipurpose framing anchors and the nails recommended by the manufacturer of the anchors *(right)*.

Nail header joists across the outside ends of the floor joists, and fasten them to the end of each joist with 2½-inch (65mm) common nails.

Lay a subfloor across the joists *(page 61)*.

Masonry Piers for Stronger Supports

Piers make a more durable foundation than wooden poles, and are almost as easy to put up. You can make them in three different ways: by pouring concrete into cylindrical fiber forms; by stacking and mortaring masonry-block piers and filling the cores of the blocks with concrete; or by setting precast piers of solid concrete.

Dealing with a Slope

As with pole platforms, piers can be used on gently sloping sites, provided the piers and their footing holes are deeper and wider than on a level site; consult a building professional. But if the slope is greater than 1 in 10—1 foot of rise for every 10 horizontal feet (1m for every 10m)—you will have to build a continuous-wall foundation *(page 48)*.

Footings

All three types of piers rest on footings—solid concrete bases that are wide and thick enough to support the structures above them. In general, a footing should be as thick as the width of a pier, and twice as wide—a pier 8 inches (200mm) wide, for example, would require a footing 8 inches (200mm) thick and 16 inches (400mm) wide. Dig the holes so the bottom of the footing is 1 foot (300mm) below ground, or 6 inches (150mm) below the frost line, whichever is deeper.

Cast Cylinders

Fiber tubes 8 inches (200mm) in diameter and 10 feet (3m) long make quick work of casting cylindrical concrete piers *(below and page 47)*; store them upright and keep them perfectly dry until they are filled. Cylindrical piers can be built to any height, making it easy to set the tops of the piers to the same level.

Masonry Blocks

These blocks come in a wide range of sizes; single-core, 8-by-12-by-12-inch (215 x 215 x 440mm) blocks make particularly sturdy piers *(page 47)*. Level the footings for block piers with a water level in the same way you level forms, but mark the height on the reinforcing bars (rebars), then measure down from the marks to set the height of the concrete for the footings.

Precast Piers

Although simple to install, these piers *(page 47)* are heavy and awkward to move and set into position. To level their footings, drive stakes into the footing holes, mark stakes with a water level as you would for concrete forms *(page 45)*, pour concrete up to the marks, and remove the stakes before the concrete begins to harden. Because they generally come no more than 18 inches (450mm) high, they are used mainly on level sites that have a shallow frost line.

Casting Concrete

Casting the footings

Locate and dig the footing-and-pier holes as for a pole platform, excavating each hole 16 inches (400mm) wide to the required depth.

At the center of each hole, drive a length of ½-inch (10mm) rebar into the ground until the top of the rod is about 6 inches (150mm) lower than the planned height of the pier above ground *(right)*.

Fill the first 8 inches (200mm) of the holes with concrete, creating footings. Allow the concrete to cure for at least one day.

Rebar

TOOLS

- Maul
- Hammer
- Tape measure (50 foot [30m])
- Plumb bob
- Power auger
- Garden spader
- Posthole digger
- Rebar cutter
- Tamper
- Carpenter's level
- Water level
- Hacksaw
- Mason's trowel

MATERIALS

- 1 x 2s (25 x 50mm), 1 x 6s (25 x 150mm), 2 x 4s (50 x 100mm)
- Pressure treated lumber (2 x 10 [50 x 250mm] or 2 x 12 [50 x 300mm])
- Galvanized common nails (3" [75mm])
- Powdered chalk
- Rebar (½" [10mm])
- Concrete mix
- Fiber forms
- Beam anchors
- Polyethylene sheeting (6-mil [heavy-duty])
- Galvanized washers
- Concrete blocks
- Precast piers
- Grout

Protect your eyes with goggles when you are hammering. Wear gloves when handling pressure-treated lumber; add a dust mask when cutting it.

Positioning the forms

Slide a form over each rebar so it rests on the footing.

Fill the hole around the form with earth, tamping it down firmly. After every 6 inches (150mm) of fill, check that the form is vertical with a carpenter's level *(right)*.

Form

Footing

Corner Form

Leveling the forms

Mark the planned height of the piers on a corner form.

Have a helper hold one end of a water level or a transparent hose filled almost completely with water at the height of the mark on the corner form.

Hold the other end against the next form in the row *(above)* and mark a line at the level of the water.

Repeat the process to mark each form.

Cut the forms at the marked heights with a hacksaw.

Embedding the anchors in concrete

With a helper and a string, go from form to form to align and mark the position of a beam anchor on the front and back of each form, ensuring that each beam—3 inches (75mm) wide for doubled 2-by-10s (50 x 250mm) or 2-by-12s (50 x 30mm), or 4½ inches (115mm) for a triple beam—will be centered on the pier.

Mix enough concrete to fill the forms, then shovel it into each form in the row, using a length of rebar to pack the concrete down with every foot you add.

As you fill each form, level the concrete off with the top of the form using a 2-by-4 (50 x 100mm), then, following the marks on the form, push an anchor that is as long as the width of the beams to be installed into the concrete down to the embedment line marked on it *(right)*.

Embed anchors in concrete in the remaining forms in the same way.

Double-check the alignment of the anchors with the string, adjusting them to line up as needed.

Allow the concrete to cure for five to seven days.

Embedment Line

Attaching the beams

Make a beam for each row of piers: For a prefab cabin, nail pairs of 2-by-10s (50 x 250mm) or 2-by-12s (50 x 30mm) together with 3-inch (75mm) galvanized common nails. Drive three nails in a row about 1 inch (25mm) from each end and stagger nails along both edges at 10-inch (250mm) intervals. For an A-frame, make triple beams.

For a vapor barrier, set asphalt shingles on the piers, or cut 6-mil (heavy-duty) polyethylene sheeting into pieces

to wrap around the bottom of the beam at each pier, and staple the pieces to the beam.

Set the beam into its anchor, then check whether it is level. If not, shim the low end by placing galvanized washers between the beam and pier.

Fasten the beam to each anchor by nailing into each hole *(above)*.

Fasten joists to the beams as for a pole foundation, then lay a subfloor across the joists.

Block and Precast Piers

Concrete-block piers

Cast a footing for each pier as for concrete piers, but level the footings by marking the rebars with a water level as for concrete forms *(page 45)*.

To keep the heights of the piers consistent, make a story pole: On a piece of lumber, mark lines at intervals equal to the height of a block plus a ⅜-inch (10mm) mortar joint.

Trowel a bed of mortar on the footing and lay a concrete block on the mortar, centering the block around the rebar.

Add blocks and mortar to build up the pier, checking each course for level and plumb with a carpenter's level *(right)*, and for height with the story pole.

Build each remaining pier in the same way, running a string between adjacent piers to keep them all consistent and in alignment.

Fill the cores of the piers with grout—concrete thinned with water so it can be poured—then embed concrete anchors in the piers and attach beams as for concrete piers.

Story Pole

Footing

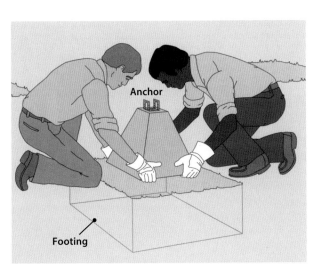

Anchor

Footing

Precast-concrete piers

Cast a footing for each pier as for concrete piers *(page 44)*, but proceed immediately, before the concrete cures.

With a helper, press a precast pier into the wet concrete *(left)*.

With a carpenter's level, ensure that the pier is level.

Position each remaining pier in the same way, running a string between adjacent ones to keep them aligned and level.

Install vapor barriers and attach beams to the piers' built-in anchors as you would for concrete piers, nailing exterior-grade plywood spacers at 24-inch (600mm) intervals between the boards making up the beam, if necessary, to ensure the beam sits snugly in the anchors.

A Continuous Block Wall

Foundations made of blocks resting on a footing of cast concrete are generally necessary in soil too unstable to support the pinpoint load of piers or poles, and in areas prone to earthquakes or hurricanes. If your cabin is in one of these areas, you will need to modify the techniques shown here. Heavy buildings such as log cabins also need this strong support. A wall foundation is easier to insulate as well, and allows plumbing to be housed in a crawl space—a must in areas with very cold winters. With some modifications, the design can be used on sites with slopes greater than 1 in 10.

Sizing the Foundation

Plan the job so the length of each foundation wall is a multiple of 8 inches (230mm)—one-half the nominal length of a standard masonry block, plus a ⅜- to ½-inch (10–12mm) mortar joint. Make the footings extend at least 12 inches (300mm) below ground—or at least 6 inches (150mm) below the frost line, whichever is deeper—and the walls rise 18 inches (450mm) above ground. For deep footings—4 feet (1.2m) or more—have a professional excavate the trenches.

Materials

To determine the number of blocks you need, multiply the total length in feet of the walls by the number of rows—called courses—then by .75. The mortar can be made from 1 part Portland cement, 1 part hydrated lime, 6 parts damp sand, and water; or by combining 1 part premixed masonry cement, 3 parts sand, and water. For a large project, it is usually easiest to have the concrete delivered in a transit-mix and poured directly into the footing. If the truck cannot reach the footing, assemble a group of helpers with wheelbarrows and plywood chutes.

TOOLS

- Maul
- Hammer
- Tape measure (50-foot [30m])
- Plumb bob
- Shovel
- Water level
- Rebar cutter
- Square-edged shovel
- Float
- Chalk line
- Mason's trowel
- Level
- Mason's line
- Tin snips
- Electric drill
- Circular saw
- Carpenter's square
- Handsaw

MATERIALS

- 1 x 2s (25 x 50mm), 1 x 6s (25 x 150mm)
- 2 x 4s (50 x 100mm), 2 x 6s (50 x 150mm)
- 2 x 8s (50 x 200mm), 2 x 10s (50 x 250mm)
- Powdered chalk
- Plywood (⅜" [9mm])
- Exterior-grade plywood (¾" [18mm])
- Ring-shank nails (2½" [65mm])
- Galvanized common nails (2½" [65mm], 3" [75mm], 3½" [100mm])
- Rebar (½" [10mm])
- Rebar supports
- Mechanic's wire (16 gauge [1.2mm])
- Concrete mix
- Polyethylene sheeting
- Mortar
- Concrete blocks
- Metal mesh
- Vents
- Anchor bolts (½" x 8" [M12 x 200mm]), washers, nuts
- Grout
- Steel plates
- Bricks

Casting the Footing

Corner Stake

Marker Stake

Locating the corners

Drive stakes at two adjacent corners of the planned foundation.

Tack nails to the tops of the stakes and stretch a string between the nails.

Drive a third stake along the line 3 feet (0.9m) from one corner and tack a nail to the stake.

Have one helper hook a tape measure on the corner-stake nail and a second helper hook another tape measure on the stake at the 3-foot (0.9m) mark. Where the 4-foot (1.2m) mark on the first tape measure crosses the 5-foot (1.5m) mark on the second, drive a marker stake *(above)*. Use this marker and the corner stake to establish the second side of the foundation.

As shown in the inset, use the same method to mark the remaining two sides.

Safety Tips

Goggles protect your eyes when you are bending rebar or hammering. Wear gloves, goggles, and a dust mask when mixing mortar and concrete. Hard-toed shoes prevent injuries from dropped blocks.

Corner Stake

Batter Board

Positioning the walls

About 5 feet (1.5m) outside the corners of the planned foundation, set up four guides—called batter boards—each built from two 1-by-6s (25 x 150mm) set at right angles and nailed to three 2-by-4 (50 x 100mm) stakes.

Stretch a string from a corner stake to the batter board at an adjacent corner and align it with the nail on the second corner stake, then mark the string's location on the batter board, defining the outside of the foundation wall *(above)*. Repeat the process to mark the outside foundation wall at each corner.

As shown in the inset, make marks on the batter boards for the inside of the foundation wall and for the trench and footing: Place a mark $7\frac{5}{8}$ inches (200mm) inside the first mark for the inside wall of the foundation. Mark the board 4 inches (100mm) outside and 12 inches (300mm) inside the first foundation mark to position the footing. For the trench, make a mark 24 inches (600mm) outside the outer footing mark and 6 inches (150mm) inside the inner footing mark.

Drive a nail at each mark and remove the corner stakes.

Batter Board — Foundation Wall

Trench — Footing

Trench-line Stake

Digging the trenches

Drive a 1-by-2 (25 x 50mm) stake into the ground in line with each trench mark on the batter boards.

Stretch strings between the stakes and trace the strings along the ground with chalk *(above)*.

Dig the trenches 8 inches (200mm) shallower than the footing depth.

Stretch strings between the footing nails on the batter boards.

Drop a plumb bob from the string to the bottom of the trench and mark lines for the footing with chalk.

Dig the footing trenches 8 inches (200mm) deeper than the trench.

Bending Rebar

To bend rebar so it follows the corners of the footing, make a bending tool from two lengths of ¾-inch (18mm) steel pipe, one 6 feet (2m) long and the other 4 feet (1.2m). Slip the rebar into the longer piece so 2 or 3 feet (60 or 100cm) of the rod protrude and set the two pieces on the ground. Place the 4-foot (1.2m) length of pipe over the projecting rebar, hold the longer pipe down with one foot, and pull the other pipe up to bend the rebar *(right)*.

Leveling the footing trench

Drive 1-by-2 (25 x 50mm) stakes into the ground at each corner of the footing trench.

Mark one stake 8 inches (200mm) from the bottom of the trench.

With a water level, transfer the mark to an adjacent corner stake *(right)*. Repeat for the three remaining corners.

Drive a pair of stakes 3 inches (75mm) from each side of the trench every 3 feet (1m).

Alternating from one side of the trench to the other, use the water level to transfer the 8-inch (200mm) marks from the corner stakes to the intermediate stakes.

Measure down from the mark on each stake to the bottom of the trench and deepen it to 8 inches (200mm) where necessary.

Make grade pegs by cutting ½-inch (10mm) rebar into 16-inch (400mm) lengths, one for each stake, with a rented rebar cutter.

Drive a peg into the trench next to each stake so the top of the peg is level with the mark on the stake.

Remove the stakes, filling in the holes they leave with soil.

Casting a reinforced footing

Set lengths of ½-inch (10mm) rebar in the trench alongside each row of grade pegs, tying concrete rebar supports to the underside of the bars at 6-foot (1.8m) intervals to hold them 3 inches (75mm) above the trench bottom. Where two bars meet end to end, overlap them 12 inches (300mm). Cut bars to length if necessary with a rented rebar cutter.

Where two pieces of the reinforcing rod meet, lash the bars together with 16-gauge (1.2mm) mechanic's wire *(left)*.

Pour concrete into the trench to just above the tops of the grade pegs, working it in with a square-edged shovel.

Level and smooth the footing with a wooden float until the tops of the pegs and footing are at the same level. If specified in the local building code, pull out the grade pegs—use pliers—and fill the holes by chopping at the concrete with a gardening trowel, then refloat the surface.

Cover the concrete with polyethylene sheeting and let it cure for seven days.

Rebar Support

Grade Peg

Building the Foundation Wall

Building the leads

Stretch strings between the outside-wall nails on the batter boards, drop a plumb bob from each line, and snap chalk lines on the footing.

Make a dry run to ensure the blocks fit.

Fashion a story pole and spread a mortar bed 10 inches (250mm) wide and 1½ inches (40mm) thick at one corner of the footing.

Lay a corner block at the intersection of two chalk lines and tap the block down with a trowel until the mortar joint is ⅜ inch (10mm) thick.

With a level, check that the block is level along its length and across its width.

Lay four blocks on each side of the corner, making the mortar joints between blocks ⅜ inch (10mm) thick, and check that they are level.

Set a corner block on top of the first one and check the height of the blocks with the story pole *(right)*.

Repeat the procedure at the three remaining corners of the footing.

Leveling the first course

Hook a mason's line between two adjacent corner blocks level with the top of the first course of blocks.

Finish laying the first course of blocks between the corners along the mason's line, adjusting the thickness of the mortar so the tops of the blocks are level with the line. If the wall will support the girder, lay one solid block instead of a hollow-core one when you reach the middle. Fill in the first course between the remaining corners in the same way, laying a second solid block opposite the first one *(left)*.

Move the mason's line up and lay the second course of blocks, making sure that the two blocks resting on a solid block in the first course are also solid.

Before spreading the mortar for the third course of blocks, use tin snips to cut a piece of metal mesh or hardware cloth two blocks long and 1 inch (25mm) wider than the cores for every pair of blocks.

Apply the mortar for the course and press the mesh into it, then lay the course. Center a solid block over each pair of solid blocks in the second course.

Solid Block

Venting the crawl space

To provide adequate ventilation for the crawl space of your structure, install one vent in the wall for every 300 square feet (30m²) of floor space. Locate vents in the fourth course of blocks, 4 feet (1.2m) from a corner. If you will be installing two vents, place them on opposite walls.

As you lay the fourth course, omit one block for each vent, and make sure that the two blocks resting on a solid block in the third course are also solid ones. When the fourth course is in place, set the vent in the mortar *(right)* so it is inset 4 inches (100mm) from the wall's outside face and the flanges on its top edge rest on the blocks to each side.

Pack mortar around the edges of the vent, sloping the mortar downward at the bottom, to shed rain.

Vent
Flange

Shelf

Forming girder pockets

Lay the fifth course like the third, but omit the mesh. Center two solid blocks over the vent and place a half block measuring 4 by 8 by 16 inches (100 x 215 x 440mm) at the middle of the girder walls so it is flush with the outside face of the wall *(left)*, leaving a 4-inch (100mm) shelf for the girder.

Setting anchor bolts

For fastening the sill plate, you need to embed ½-by-8-inch (M12 x 200mm) L-shaped anchor bolts in the blocks. Locate bolts 10 inches (250mm) from each corner and every 20 inches (500mm) along the walls in between. In a high-wind area, you can embed bolts for anchor-downs to reinforce the structure.

Make a positioning jig for each bolt by drilling a ⅝-inch (15mm) hole through the middle of a 1-foot-long (300mm) 2-by-6 (50 x 150mm).

Fill the cores of all the blocks with grout—concrete thinned with water so it can be poured—and trowel it flush with their tops.

Slip an anchor bolt through its hole in a jig and thread a washer and nut onto the bolt about 1 inch (25mm) from the threaded end. Position the jig on the wall flush with the outside faces of the blocks and tap the bolt into the grout so the washer is flat against the jig *(right)*.

After 24 hours, remove the nuts, washers, and positioning jigs. Set the nuts and washers aside.

Anchor Bolt

Positioning Jig

A Stepped Foundation for Sloping Sites

For sites with a slope greater than 1 in 10—1 vertical foot for every 10 horizontal feet (1m for every 10m)—you will need to adapt the design of a continuous-wall foundation (page 48). This can be done by casting stepped footings for the walls that follow the slope (below). Because of local variations due to such factors as different soil types, have your plan checked by a building-code official in the area, or a contractor familiar with local custom before you start to dig.

The walls at the top and bottom of the slope are built in the standard fashion, but the walls along the slope need stepped footing trenches. Dig the trenches so each step is a multiple of 8 inches (200mm) deep. The number of steps you need depends on the difference in elevation between the high and low ends of the footing; a 4-foot (1.2m) difference on a mild slope, for example, would require five 8-inch (200mm) steps. On a steeper slope the steps could be 16 (400mm) or 24 inches (600mm).

Footing — Rebar Support — Rebar Overlap — Rebar — 8" — 8" — 24"

To contain the concrete for the footing within the steps, build a series of wooden forms (right). Place the form boards for the front of the steps at least 24 inches (600mm)—or the distance required by the building code or local custom—in front of the forward edge of the trench step. To make form boards for 8-inch-high (200mm) steps, cut 2-by-8s (50 x 200mm) to length and tack on strips of ½-inch (12mm) plywood cut 1½ inches (40mm) wide. Anchor them at the sides with stakes so the tops of the boards are level and 8 inches (200mm) above the bottom of the trench. Fasten them together with 3½-inch (100mm), easy-to-remove double-headed nails.

Cut ½-inch (10mm) rebar into lengths that can be bent to overlap at the middle of each step by at least 12 inches (300mm), and anchor the rods with rebar supports and wire. When the

concrete has cured, remove the form boards and stakes, and erect the block wall.

Plywood — 24" — 8" — Form Board — Grade Stake

From Sill Plate to Girder

Fastening the sill plate

Cut a 2-by-6 (50 x 150mm) to the length of one foundation wall to make a sill plate.

With a helper holding the plate against the anchor bolts on the wall so the ends are flush with the corners, use a carpenter's square to mark a line across the plate at the center of each anchor bolt *(above)*.

Measure the distance from the outside edge of the wall to the center of the bolt, transfer this point to each marked line, and drill a ¾-inch (20mm) hole through the sill plate at each point.

Slip the sill plate over the bolts and fasten it with the washers and nuts.

Attach sill plates atop the three remaining walls in the same way, then toenail the ends of the boards together with 3-inch (75mm) galvanized common nails.

Above each girder pocket, cut a 1½- by-5¾-inch (40 x 145mm) notch into the inside edge of the sill plate.

Girder Pocket

Notch

Locating the girder piers

Stretch a string between nails tacked into the sill plates above the center of each girder pocket.

With a helper stretching a 50-foot (30m) tape measure along the string, hang rags from the tape to divide the distance between the nails into thirds *(above)*.

Drop a plumb bob from each rag and mark the ground for piers.

Erect a masonry-block or cast-concrete pier at each location so its top is level with the bottoms of the girder pockets.

Remove the nails and strings.

Making and placing the girder

Cut three 2-by-10s (50 x 250mm) to fit between the notches in the sill plates, less 1 inch (25mm). Using the nailing pattern prescribed for doubled beams, form the boards into a girder by nailing them together *(right)*. If the span of the girder will exceed 16 feet (4.8m), splice 2-by-10s (50 x 250mm) end to end so the seams will sit on the piers.

With a helper for every 5 feet (1.5m) of girder length, set the girder in its notches and on the piers, leaving ½ inch (12mm) of space between the ends of the girders and the backs of its notches.

Check that the top of the girder is flush with the top of the sill plate; add steel plates or slate shims, if necessary.

Fill empty spaces in the girder pocket with bricks cut in half. Leave ⅜-inch (10mm) mortar joints between the bricks and a ½"-inch (12mm) gap on each side of the girder.

Masonry-block Pier

Girder Splice

Adding a Floor

Marking the sill plates for joists

Tack a nail into the sill plate 15½ inches (390mm) from the end of a long wall.

Have a helper hook a tape measure on the nail, then mark joist locations on the sill plate at 16-inch (400mm) intervals, drawing lines on both sides of the leg of a carpenter's square *(right)*.

Repeat the marking procedure on the opposite-wall sill plate.

Transfer the joist locations from the plates to the girder with a chalk line.

If you are building a log cabin, omit header and stringer joists. Once the sill logs are in place, install floor joists, a vapor barrier, and a subfloor.

Header Joist

Joist Location

Band Joist

Nailing header and band joists

With a helper, set a 2-by-10 (50 x 250mm) band joist on the marked sill plate, outside face flush with the outside of the wall, and toenail it to the plate with 2½-inch (65mm) galvanized common nails.

Position a 2-by-10 (50 x 250mm) header joist on the adjacent sill plate, butt it against the band joist, and nail the joists together with 3½-inch (100mm) galvanized nails *(above)*.

Fasten header and band joists together and to the remaining two plates in the same manner.

With a carpenter's square, extend the joist-location lines from the sill plates to the inside faces of the header joists.

Filling in with joists

Measure and cut 2-by-10 (50 x 250mm) joists to fit between one header joist and the middle of the girder.

Set the first joist on the sill plate, aligned with its location marks, and nail it to the header joist.

Toenail the joist to the girder.

Fasten the first joist to the opposite header joist in the same way, then secure the seam between the joists by nailing a 9¼-inch (235mm) square of ⅜-inch (9mm) plywood to each side *(above)*.

Attach the next pair of joists in the same manner.

Laying a vapor barrier

Unroll a length of 3-foot-wide (at least a meter wide) 6-mil (heavy-duty) polyethylene sheeting on the ground under the first two joists *(right)*.

Weigh down the corners of the sheeting with brick or stones.

Fasten two more joists and set down more sheeting, overlapping the first layer by 6 inches (150mm). Continue in this fashion until the last of the joists is fastened.

Laying the subfloor

Cut 2-by-8s (50 x 200mm) into 16-inch (400mm) lengths of blocking.

Nail the blocking between the joists at 4-foot (1.2m) intervals.

Starting at one corner of the foundation, lay a ¾-inch (18mm) exterior-grade plywood panel atop the joists—long edges perpendicular to the joists.

Fasten the panel to the joists and blocking with 2½-inch (65mm) ring-shank nails spaced 6 inches (150mm) apart around its perimeter, and 12 inches (300mm) along the joists *(left)*.

Nail down the rest of the floor in the same way, leaving a ⅛-inch (3mm) gap all around each panel. Stagger the end joints between rows of panels—cutting the first sheets of each row in half if necessary.

Blocking

Chapter 3

FOUR SIMPLE STRUCTURES

Esthetic preferences or personal lifestyles may be guiding factors when you are deciding on a cabin design. Whether you want a sophisticated chalet or a rustic retreat, you can begin with one of the four basic structures shown on the following pages. All can be built by an amateur with a minimum of special skills and tools, and each can suit a particular taste or solve a special construction problem.

A Cottage of Prefab Panels

The vacation house most like a year-round home has standard stud walls covered with siding *(page 69)*. An advantage to this structure is that its walls can be prefabricated in sections, hauled to the site in a small truck, and, with three or four helpers, quickly assembled on the floor of the cabin and topped with a simple rafter or truss roof *(page 95)*.

Planning

To ensure that the sections fit together properly, draw a scaled plan of the structure before building the panels. Indicate the size of the foundation and the location and dimensions of walls, doors, and windows. You can simplify construction by ordering doors and windows that fit between studs *(opposite)*. If you are planning to build your cabin with a shed roof *(page 90)*, you'll need to make the back wall higher than the front, or one side wall higher than the other.

Wall Panels

The wall frames are built in multiples of 4 feet (1.2m)—a size that suits common building materials. The economical cabin shown on these pages uses 8-foot (2.4m) exterior siding, and has ceilings just under 7 feet (2.1m) high. If you want higher ceilings, cut the wall studs longer and buy 10-foot (3m) siding (if available)—which costs a bit more—and trim it to length.

Place the assembled panels on the truck in order so that the last one you load is the first to be erected; this way, you can unload and assemble the walls in sequence.

If you are building the cabin in an area prone to earthquakes or hurricanes, you will need to modify some of the techniques shown in this section.

TOOLS

- Sawhorses
- Screwdriver
- Circular saw
- Electric drill
- Saber saw
- Hammer
- Tin snips
- Cold chisel
- Carpenter's square
- Carpenter's level
- Maul
- Chalk line

MATERIALS

- 1 x 3s (25 x 75mm), 1 x 4s (25 x 100mm), 1 x 6s (25 x 150mm)
- 2 x 2s (50 x 50mm), 2 x 4s (50 x 100mm), 2 x 6s (50 x 150mm)
- Plywood (½" [12mm])
- Common nails (2" [50mm], 3" [75mm], 3½" [100mm])
- Galvanized common and box nails (2" [50mm])
- Galvanized finishing nails (2¼" [60mm])
- Wood screws (2" [50mm] No. 6 [3.5mm])
- Hinges
- Exterior plywood siding (⅝" [15mm])
- Aluminum flashing (6" [150mm])

Partition Wall

Siding

Overlapping Top Plate

Basic Panel

Blocking

Filler Panel

Modified Basic Panel

Nailing Stud

Anatomy of a prefab cabin

This 20- by 24-foot (6 x 7.2m) cabin has wall panels in three sizes. (For clarity, some panels are shown without siding.) The basic panels are 8 feet (2.4m) wide, the filler and corner panels are 4 feet (1.2m) wide. Modified basic panels at each corner provide a nailing surface for the end stud of the adjoining corner panel. The wall sections are nailed together where they abut, and connected by an overlapping top plate, installed on site. Interior partition walls are framed the same way as the exterior walls, which have blocking where the partitions adjoin them. Any foundation or roof can be used.

Safety Tips

Goggles protect eyes from injury when you are using power tools or hammering.

The basic panel

Each panel is made from seven 2-by-4 (50 x 100mm) studs cut 6 feet 9 inches (2030mm) long. The 2-by-4 (50 x 100mm) top and soleplates are cut 8 feet (2.4m) long, and the studs are fastened to the plates at 16-inch (400mm) intervals with the middle stud in the center of the panel so wallboard and interior paneling can be nailed there. Two pieces of ⅝-inch (15mm) vertical siding are nailed to the studs and plates flush with the outside faces of the outer studs so they project above the top plate by 1½ inches (40mm) and below the soleplate by 10½ inches (265mm).

Filler panels are made in the same way, but with four studs and one piece of siding, so they are only 4 feet (1.2m) wide. A basic panel can be adapted to accommodate a window or door as shown for the modified and corner panels below.

A modified basic panel

To tie walls together at a corner, an extra "nailer" stud is added—flush with the inside edge of the soleplate—at the left end of a basic panel—when viewed from the outside—to serve as a nailing surface for the first stud of the adjoining corner panel. For a panel with a window opening, a header, made with ½-inch (12mm) plywood nailed between two 2-by-6s (50 x 150mm), spans the top of the opening; jack studs nailed to the king studs at either side of the opening support the header; a rough sill is toenailed to the jack studs; and a cripple stud braces the rough sill.

A corner panel

The top and soleplates of this panel are 7 feet 8½ inches (2345mm) long, with the stud at the corner spaced only 12½ inches (320mm) from the next stud. The sheathing overlaps the corner end by 3½ inches (90mm). When the panel is put in place, the overlapped siding attaches to the end stud of a modified basic panel. Because the siding always overlaps to the right when viewed from outside, erect the walls from left to right. A door opening is framed much like that of a window, but the rough sill and cripple stud are omitted.

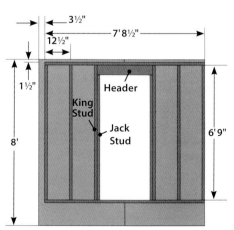

Building Walls in Sections

Saw Guide

Side Stop

End Stop

Sizing the studs with a jig

To make a jig that will enable you to cut several studs to length in a single operation, secure a plywood panel atop a pair of sawhorses with 2-inch (50mm) common nails. With 3-inch (75mm) nails, attach a 2-by-4 (50 x 100mm) stop along one side of the panel, and a 2-by-2 (50 x 50mm) stop along an end, perpendicular to the side stop. With a hinge, fasten a 2-by-2 (50 x 50mm) guide at a 90-degree angle across the side stop and panel; locate the guide so that the studs will be the correct length when you run a circular saw along it.

Swing the saw guide up and put the 2-by-4s (50 x 100mm) edge to edge in the jig so they are butted against the end stop and the first board is flush against the side stop. Lower the guide in place.

Holding the 2-by-4s (50 x 100mm) steady, run a circular saw across the boards with the base plate against the guide *(above)*.

Soleplate

Nailer Stud

Top Plate

Joining the studs and plates

Cut the top and soleplates to length, then mark stud locations on one face of each board, placing the middle-stud mark in the center of each plate and the rest at 16-inch (400mm) intervals. If the panel will have a window or door opening, space the studs on each side of the gap according to the rough opening required, plus 3 inches (75mm).

To join the studs and top plate, align the stud with its outline, stand on the board, and drive two 3½-inch (100m) common nails through the plate into the stud *(left)*.

Attach the soleplate the same way.

Header

Rough Sill

King Stud

Cripple Stud

Jack Stud

Framing a rough opening for a window

To make the header, first cut two 2-by-6s (50 x 150mm) and a ½-inch (12mm) plywood spacer of the same width to fit in the opening; sandwich the spacer between the 2-by-6s (50 x 150mm) and secure the assembly with 3½-inch (100mm) common nails driven every 10 inches (250mm) in a staggered pattern.

Cut two jack studs to fit between the header and soleplate, and fasten them to the king studs at each side of the opening.

Cut a 2-by-4 (50 x 100mm) rough sill to fit between the jack studs and fasten it (above), spacing it from the header the distance indicated by the window manufacturer's specifications.

Cut a 2-by-4 (50 x 100mm) cripple stud to fit between the sill and soleplate, then nail it to both boards.

Frame a door opening in the same way, but omit the sill and cripple stud.

2 × 4 Stop

1 × 6 Stops

2 × 2 Stop

A jig for fastening the siding

Cut a 2-by-2 (50 x 50mm) stop 8 feet (2.4m) long and nail it along one edge of a plywood panel.

Cut a 2-by-4 (50 x 100mm) stop 3 feet 10½ inches (1165mm) long and fasten it along an end of the panel.

Cut two 1-by-6s (25 x 150mm) to the lengths of the two stops; then, with 2-inch (50mm) No. 6 (3.5mm) wood screws, fasten one to the inside edge of the 2-by-4 (50 x 100mm) and the other to the outside of the 2-by-2 (50 x 50mm).

Adding siding to basic panels

Set the siding jig on the floor and place the panel on it so the top plate rests flush against the 2-by-2 (50 x 50mm) stop and an outer stud sits against the shorter 1-by-6 (25 x 150mm) stop.

Place a sheet of ⅝-inch (15mm) exterior siding atop the panel so one end and edge are butted against the 1-by-6 inch (25 x 150mm) stops.

With 2½-inch (65mm) galvanized box nails, fasten the siding to the top, soleplates, and studs, leaving ⅛ inch (3mm) between panels and driving the fasteners at 6-inch (150mm) intervals around the perimeter and every 12 inches (300mm) along the studs *(above)*.

If the panel has a window or door opening, turn it over and drill a hole through the sheathing at each corner of the opening. Join the holes with pencil lines and cut the siding along the marks with a saber saw.

Covering end panels

Modify the jig by moving the shorter 1-by-6 (25 x 150mm) from the inside to the outside of the 2-by-4 (50 x 100mm) stop *(inset)*. Nail the siding to the frame *(left)*.

Flashing an opening

With tin snips, cut a piece of 6-inch (150mm) aluminum flashing to the width of the rough opening.

Bend the aluminum over a 2-by-4 (50 x 100mm) to a 90-degree angle, forming two flanges.

Loosen the siding around the header with a cold chisel or pry bar.

Slip one flange of the flashing between the header and the paneling *(right)*, then nail the flashing and siding to the header.

Nailer Stud

Brace

Erecting the Panels

Bracing the first panel

Have two helpers hold a modified basic panel plumb at one end of the foundation, positioning the nailer stud at the corner.

With 3½-inch (100mm) common nails, attach a 2-by-4 (50 x 100mm) brace to the second stud, fasten a short board to the bottom of the brace, and nail the board to the subfloor *(left)*.

Fasten a brace at the other end of the panel to hold it plumb.

Anchor the panel to the foundation by nailing its soleplate to the subfloor, driving a nail through the plate between each pair of studs.

Extending the wall

Position the second panel against the first.

With a helper holding the panel upright, use a 4-pound maul to align it with the first *(above)*.

Plumb and brace the second panel, then nail the abutting joists of the two panels together.

Repeat the process to raise three of the four walls, working from left to right (when viewed from outside the cabin) so each corner has a modified panel and an overlapping corner panel.

Bring the interior walls inside, then raise the fourth wall.

With 2-inch (50mm) galvanized nails, fasten the sheathing of the corner panels to the nailer studs of the modified panels.

Modified Panel

Overlapping Top Plate

Corner Panel

Tying the walls together

Cut a 2-by-4 (50 x 100mm) top plate 4 feet (1.2m) long and, with 3½-inch (100mm) nails, fasten it atop the top plate of a corner panel so it overlaps the top plate of a modified panel *(left)*.

Continue in this fashion around the perimeter of the wall, nailing on 8-foot-long (2.4m) plates that overlap the seams between adjacent panels. Cut the last 2-by-4 (50 x 100mm) of each wall to fit against the adjoining wall.

Working outside, cover the exposed edges of the siding with 1-by-3s (25 x 75mm) and 1-by-4s (25 x 100mm) fastened with 2¼-inch (60mm) galvanized finishing nails. Nail on the 1-by-4 (25 x 100mm) first so it overlaps the corner by ¾ inch (20mm), then attach the 1-by-3 (25 x 75mm) flush against the 1-by-4 (25 x 100mm).

Raising Partitions

Locating the wall

With a helper at each side wall, snap a chalk line across the subfloor at one side of the proposed wall. To locate a wall directly above the girder, measure the distance between one foundation wall and the girder from below the floor, then transfer the measurement to the floor.

Snap a parallel line 3½ inches (90mm) from the first *(left)*.

Erecting the wall

Cut six 2-by-4 (50 x 100mm) blocks to fit between the studs on each side of the chalk lines on the subfloor.

With 3½-inch (100mm) common nails, fasten three pieces of blocking to each wall, one near the bottom, one at the middle, and one near the top *(left)*.

Raise the interior wall as you did the exterior ones.

Fasten the outer studs of the first and last interior-wall panels to the blocking.

Nail together the end studs of the wall panels, then tie the panels together.

The A-Frame: A String of Sturdy Triangles

One of the sturdiest of all structures is the A-frame, whose skeleton consists simply of a row of triangles. The bases of the triangles are the joists that support the floor, and the sides are the rafters that hold the combined walls and roof. The simplicity of construction and comparatively low cost make it a popular choice for vacation cabins. Any style of foundation can serve as its base.

structure like the one on these pages, three people can lift the assembled triangles into place without the assistance of special equipment; a structure with rafters greater than 24 feet (7m) may prove too unwieldy for a crew of amateurs. Frame doors and windows in the end walls; for a large A-frame, plan a lot of windows to keep the interior from being too dark.

Planning the Structure

The most common shape is equilateral—joists and rafters are equal in length and set at angles of 60 degrees to each other; however, you can use different angles to modify the shape (chart, page 74). An A-frame can be built to almost any size simply by varying the number of triangles and their dimensions, but a cabin with a sleeping loft must have rafters at least 20 feet (6m) long to allow adequate headroom on both floors. For a small

Finishing Touches

If the A-frame includes a loft (page 81), provide it with stairs or a ladder, and a sturdy railing. Rest a deck, if you build one, on the same foundation as the main structure and surround it with a railing (page 83). Buy deck stairs at a building center or construct them on site. Install insulation between the floor joists, rafters, and end-wall studs as you build.

TOOLS

- Screwdriver
- Circular saw
- C-clamps
- Electric drill
- Hammer
- Carpenter's level
- Carpenter's square
- Plumb bob
- Wrench
- Saber saw

MATERIALS

- 1 x 2s (25 x 50mm), 2 x 4s (50 x 100mm)
- 2 x 6s (50 x 150mm), 2 x 8s (50 x 200mm)
- Pressure-treated 22 x 6s (50 x 150mm), 2 x 10s (50 x 250mm), 4 x 4s (100 x 100mm)
- Exterior-grade plywood (¾" [18mm])
- Wood glue

- Common nails (2" [50mm], 2½" [65mm], 3½" [100mm])
- Galvanized common nails (2½" [65mm], 3" [75mm], 3½" [100mm])
- Ring-shank nails (2½" [65mm])
- Wood screws (1¾" [45mm] No. 8 [4mm])
- Roofing materials

- Carriage bolts (⅝" x 6" [M16 x 150mm], ½" x 4" [M12 x 100mm], ½" x 6" [M12 x 150mm])
- Lag screws (½" x 4" [M12 x 100])
- Multipurpose and framing anchors and nails
- Wooden ladder
- Concrete mix

Safety Tips

Protect your eyes with goggles when using power tools or hammering. Wear gloves when handling pressure-treated lumber; add a dust mask when cutting it.

Common Floor-to-Rafter Angles

Rafter Length	Joist Length	Rafter/Joist Angle	Rafter/Rafter Angle
16' (4.8m)	12' (3.5m)	68°	22°
16' (4.8m)	14' (4.25m)	64.1°	26°
16' (4.8m)	16' (4.8m)	60°	30°
20' (6m)	12' (3.5m)	72.5°	17.5°
20' (6m)	14' (4.25m)	69.5°	20.5°
20' (6m)	16' (4.8m)	66.4°	23.6°
20' (6m)	20' (6m)	60°	30°

Anatomy of an A-frame

This 20-foot-per-side (6m) equilateral A-frame rests on tripled 2-by-10 (50 x 250mm) pressure-treated beams supported by masonry-block piers. The triangles, spaced 24 inches (600mm) apart, are formed of 2-by-8 (50 x 200mm) rafters joined at the apexes with plywood gussets and sandwiched at the bottom by pairs of pressure-treated 2-by-6 (50 x 150mm) joists. (A cabin larger than this structure would require correspondingly larger framing lumber.) At the end walls and under the sleeping loft, horizontal 2-by-6 (50 x 150mm) collar beams are fastened between the rafters. The rafters of the end walls are doubled to provide a flush nailing surface for the exterior sheathing. The sleeping loft, reached by a ladder, is framed by a railing secured to posts and rafters. Knee walls along the sides of the cabin provide concealed storage areas. The deck rests on 2-by-6 (50 x 150mm) joists set 16 inches (400mm) apart. Posts for the railing are secured to the deck joists; the stairs are set on concrete footings and are attached to the deck with metal framing anchors. All exposed wood is pressure-treated lumber. Although an asphalt-shingle roof is shown, any of the roofing alternatives in this book *(page 98)* could be installed.

Rafter

Doubled Rafter

Gusset

Post

Collar Beam

Railing

Knee-wall Stud

Beam

Joist

Masonry-block Pier

Multi-purpose Framing Anchor

Deck Post

Deck Post

Footing

Erecting the Skeleton

Cutting joists and rafters

To cut the joists and rafters quickly, make a jig for each angle to be cut.

Mark a scrap board at the angle of the joists or rafters and set it on a work surface.

Place a 2-by-4 (50 x 100mm) on each side of the board and fasten them down with screws.

Align a 1-by-2 (25 x 50mm) with the mark and screw it to the 2-by-4s (50 x 100mm) as a cutting guide.

Run a circular saw along the guide, cutting a kerf through all three boards.

Remove the scrap board and replace it with a joist or rafter, marked to length. Align the mark with the kerf and cut the board (right). Cut the other end so both cuts angle toward the middle.

Stop

Kerf

Guide

Easy Angles with a Miter Saw

A power miter saw can cut joists and rafters to the appropriate angles without the need of a jig. The model shown at left features a radial arm that allows the blade to slide back and forth for wide stock. Simply swivel the base of the saw to the desired angle and lock it in place. Hold the board against the base and fence with the blade. Keeping your hand safely away from the blade, squeeze the trigger, and lower the blade over the board. For big jobs, set the saw on sawhorses or a couple of concrete blocks.

Base

Fence

Assembling the triangles

Clamp the ends of two joists around the base of a rafter, aligning the ends and edges of the boards, and drill a ⅝-inch (15mm) hole through the three layers *(right)*.

Fasten the boards together with a ⅝- by 6-inch (M16 x 150mm) carriage bolt, washer, and nut.

Bolt the opposite ends of the joists to the base of another rafter in the same way.

From ¾-inch (18mm) exterior grade plywood, cut two triangular gussets to the same angle as the A-frame.

Butt the top ends of the rafters together and fasten the gussets to each side of the seam with wood glue and 1¾-inch (45mm) No. 8 (4mm) wood screws *(inset)*.

Add a second carriage bolt to each joist-rafter joint.

Assemble the remaining triangles in the same way, but secure gussets to just one side of each end triangle.

Allowing for at least 7 feet (2.1m) of headroom, mark both rafters of each triangle at the end walls and under the loft for collar beams. For each triangle, cut two collar beams to fit between the outside edges of the rafters, then bolt them on as you did the joists.

Cut 1-by-2 (25 x 50mm) spacers to the joist width and fasten them with 2-inch (50mm) common nails between all the pairs of joists and collar beams at 2-foot (600mm) intervals.

Double the rafters of the end triangles: Cut four lengths of rafter lumber—two to fit between the joists and collar and two between the beams and rafter peaks—and nail them to the outsides of the rafters with 2½-inch (65mm) nails.

Joists

Rafter

Erecting the triangles

Mark the triangle locations on the beams at 2-foot (600mm) intervals.

Nail scabs—1-foot-long (300mm) 2-by-4s (50 x 100mm)—to the insides of the outer beams on each side of the marks for the front end triangle.

With a pair of helpers, lift and position the end triangle on the beam between the scabs.

Plumb the triangle and brace it with two 2-by-4s (50 x 100mm) nailed diagonally between the rafters and outer beams so the top of each brace is least 4½ feet (1.35m) from the base of the rafters.

Position and plumb the remaining triangles in the same way, bracing them with a 1-by-2 (25 x 50mm) nailed to each side of the adjacent triangle *(right)*.

When all the triangles are braced, remove the scabs and attach the triangles to the beams, installing a multipurpose framing anchor to each side of every joist. In a high-wind area, use hurricane ties. Nail the bottom corners of the triangles to the beams.

Sheathe the outside of the frame, laying decking for shakes, or 4-by-8 (1.2 x 2.4m) panels of ⅝-inch (15mm) exterior-grade plywood for metal roofing *(page 99)* or asphalt shingles *(page 101)*. Work from bottom to top, fastening the sheathing with 2½-inch (65mm) common nails. Leave a ⅛-inch (3mm) gap around panels and stagger the joints. Remove the bracing after you lay the bottom course of panels.

Cover the floor with plywood.

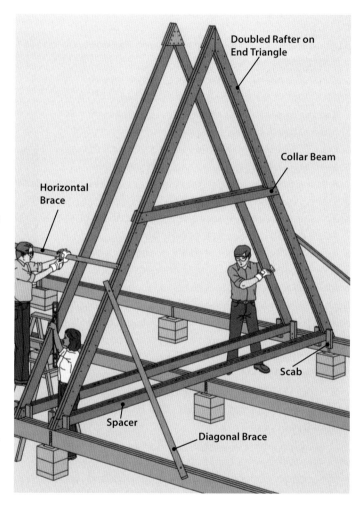

Doubled Rafter on End Triangle

Collar Beam

Horizontal Brace

Scab

Spacer

Diagonal Brace

Framing the Ends

Making the plates

Cut a 2-by-4 (50 x 100mm) soleplate to fit between the rafters at each end of the floor, and fasten them in place with 2½-inch (65mm) common nails spaced 16 inches (400mm) apart.

Cut a top plate to fit under the collar beam directly above each soleplate.

Set a top plate against its soleplate, centered between the longer board's ends, and use a carpenter's square to mark a stud location every 16 inches (400mm) across both boards *(right)*. Mark the other top plate in the same way.

Raising the end walls

Cut studs to fit between the top and soleplates and toenail them to the top plate, framing doors or windows *(above)* as for a prefabricated frame cottage, but using 2-by-4s (50 x 100mm) for headers and fastening cripple studs between the headers and top plates.

With helpers, tilt each wall upright and set the studs on their marks on the soleplate.

Keeping the wall plumb with a carpenter's level, toenail each stud to the soleplate with 3-inch (75mm) nails and fasten the top plate to the underside of its collar beam.

Attaching the mitered studs

Set a 2-by-4 (50 x 100mm) on the floor against the soleplate.

Stand a 2-by-4 (50 x 100mm) stud on the board in line with one of the unoccupied stud marks, hold it plumb, and mark a line across its face along the bottom edge of the rafters *(right)*.

Cut the stud to length and toenail it to the rafters and the soleplate.

Frame the remaining portions of the walls above and below the collar beams in the same way.

Sheathe the outside of the end walls with ¾-inch (18mm) exterior-grade plywood.

Putting in Knee Walls

Framing the walls

Cut two 2-by-4 (50 x 100mm) soleplates to fit between the end-wall plates and position one along each side wall at a distance that will create a useful storage area behind the knee wall without cutting off too much floor space.

Hang a plumb bob from each rafter in turn and mark the soleplate for studs.

Mark and miter a stud as described in Step 3 above, then use it as a template to trim the remaining studs.

Fasten the studs to the soleplate with 3½-inch (100mm) common nails, tilt the frame into position, and nail the plate to the floor and the studs to the rafters with 2½-inch (65mm) nails *(right)*.

Finishing the Loft

Bolting railing posts

In the loft, mark locations for 2-by-4 (50 x 100mm) posts on the outside face of the front collar beam to either side of the place you plan to put the ladder.

Cut the posts to fit between the bottom of the beam and the top of the rafters directly above.

Cut 2-by-4 (50 x 100mm) blocking to fit between each post and rafter.

Clamp the post to the beam, drill a ⅜-inch (9mm) hole through the post and into the beam, and attach the post with a ½-by-4-inch (M12 x 100mm) lag screw.

Plumb the post, drill through the post, blocking, and rafter, and secure the assembly with two ½-by-6-inch (M12 x 150mm) carriage bolts.

Add a second lag screw to the bottom of each post *(right)*.

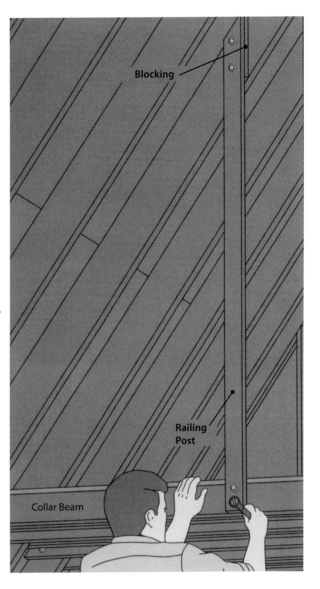

Blocking

Railing Post

Collar Beam

Attaching the railing

Cut a 2-by-4 (50 x 100mm) railing to span between the outside edges of each post and rafter 3 feet (1m) above the loft floor; miter one end of the board to match the roof slope.

Fasten the railing to the back of the railing post and to the front of the rafter with two ½-by-6-inch (M12 x 150mm) carriage bolts at each location (*above*).

Add two more rails to each post spaced no more than 6 inches (150mm) apart.

Fasten a wooden ladder to the collar beam with framing anchors.

A Folding Ladder to the Loft

To save floor space downstairs, install a folding ladder to access the loft. For the model shown at left, frame an opening in the loft floor by fastening headers between adjacent collar beams and adding blocking between the headers; use collar beam–size lumber for the headers and blocking. Attach the ladder, which comes mounted to a frame, to the framing according to the manufacturer's instructions.

Blocking

Frame

Headers

Building a Deck

Laying the understructure

With multipurpose framing anchors, fasten a 2-by-6 (50 x 150mm) deck joist cut as long as the cabin's width across the beams, flush against the outer joist of the first triangle. If the width exceeds 20 feet (6m), splice two shorter joists over the middle girder.

Attach a joist every 16 inches (400mm) until you reach the beams' ends.

Cut two 2-by-6 (50 x 150mm) perimeter boards to fit against the ends of the deck joists. Attach the boards along the sides of the deck with 3½-inch (100mm) galvanized common nails (left); fasten their inside faces to the joists with framing anchors.

Installing railing posts

Set a 3½-foot-long (1.05m) pressure-treated 4-by-4 (100 x 100mm) post on the beam at each corner of the deck and clamp it securely.

Drill a hole through the perimeter board into each post and two holes through the deck joist for ½-by-4-inch (M12 x 100mm) carriage bolts and fasten the post in place (right).

Bolt two posts to the inside of the outer deck joist on either side of the stairway opening, resting one post on the middle beam, if possible. Brace the posts by nailing 2-by-6 (50 x 150mm) blocking between adjacent joists and bolting the posts to the blocking.

With 3-inch (75mm) galvanized common nails or No. 8 (4mm) wood screws, fasten 2-by-6 (50 x 150mm) decking boards spaced ¼ inch (6mm) apart across the joists; notch the decking, as necessary, to fit around the railing posts.

Completing the rail

Cut 2-by-4 (50 x 100mm) rails to fit along the outsides of adjacent posts.

With 2½-inch (65mm) galvanized common nails, fasten bottom rails to the outside faces of the posts at the distance from the decking specified by local code—typically no more than 4 to 6 inches (100–150mm).

Attach two sets of middle rails and a top rail to the posts at the same intervals, mitering the ends of the top rails that meet over the posts.

To enclose the corners of the deck at the end wall, first screw 3-foot-long (1m) rails to each corner post and nail them to studs in the end wall. Then, cut a notch in the decking with a saber saw to accommodate a 4-by-4 (100 x 100mm) post and bolt the post to the joist. Add a top rail and toenail the post to the bottom and middle rails *(right)*.

Mounting stairs

Pour a concrete footing to support the bottom of each stair stringer—the diagonal board that runs along the sides of the steps.

Fasten the tops of the stringers to the outer deck joists with framing anchors *(left)*.

Bolt a 4-by-4 (100 x 100mm) bottom post to the outside of each stringer with two ½-by-6-inch (M12 x 150mm) carriage bolts so the post rests on the footing.

Cut 2-by-4 (50 x 100mm) handrails to fit between the bottom posts and the deck posts 2 inches (50mm) below the top rails.

With 3½-inch (100mm) galvanized nails, fasten the handrails to the posts parallel with the stringers.

A House Suspended on Poles

Building a pole-frame cabin is not much different from erecting a pole-platform foundation *(page 39)*. In each case, pressure-treated poles are anchored in the ground and horizontal beams are bolted to them to support an understructure that serves as both foundation and floor. The pole-frame cabin requires longer poles on the sides to support additional beams for the roof, and the outer beams on the outside poles are omitted. The resulting structure is a rustic but sturdy vacation home that has even greater resistance to storms and floods than one that simply rests on a platform.

Building the Understructure

A one-story cabin is built around two outside rows of 15-foot (4.5m) poles and one or more middle rows of 6- to 7-foot (1.8–2.1m) poles, all sunk and secured like those of a pole platform *(page 39)*, and spaced no more than 8 feet (2.4m) apart. For a shed roof *(page 91)*, taller poles are needed on one side. For a structure up to 16 feet (4.8m) wide, one middle row is needed and single 16-foot 2-by-10s (4800 x 50 x 250mm) serve as support beams. For a wider or longer cabin requiring additional poles, use shorter joists or beams and overlap them at the intermediate poles. Rent metal scaffolding to install the eave beams, and work with at least two helpers to set the heavy and cumbersome outside poles.

Bracing and Aligning the Poles

After you have set the poles in the ground, the techniques of bracing and aligning them vary only slightly from those used for the pole platform. Plumb the inner surfaces of the side poles by placing a long straight board against the pole and a 4-foot (1.2m) level on the board. As you plumb each pole, brace it two-thirds of the way up. When you cut daps in the outside poles for floor beams, you will have to complete the recesses with a wood chisel. Cutting daps for the eave beams can be handled entirely with a saw. Once these supports are in place, the cabin is ready to be walled *(page 110)* and roofed *(page 98)*. When raising the walls, trim corner panels to fit against the middle poles and caulk the seams between the panels and the poles.

TOOLS

- Power auger
- Shovel
- Posthole digger
- Carpenter's level
- Circular saw
- Hammer
- 2 x 4 (50 x 100mm) tamper
- Bucksaw
- Wood chisel
- Mallet
- Combination square
- Electric drill
- Auger bit (½" [12mm])
- Wrench

MATERIALS

- 1 x 2s (25 x 50mm)
- Pressure-treated poles (6"–8" [150–200mm] thick: 2 x 6s [50 x 150mm], 2 x 8s [50 x 200mm], 2 x 10s [50 x 250mm])
- Exterior-grade plywood (¾" [18mm])
- Common nails (1½" [40mm], 3" [75mm])
- Ring-shank nails (2½" [65mm])
- Carriage bolts (½" [M12]), washers, nuts
- Multipurpose framing anchors and nails
- Concrete mix
- Siding and roofing materials

Safety Tips

Goggles protect your eyes when you are hammering and using power tools. Wear gloves when handling pressure-treated lumber; add a dust mask when cutting it.

Eave Beam

Subfloor

Floor Joist

Blocking

Middle Pole

Concrete Jacket

Outside Pole

Floor Beam

Anatomy of a pole-suspended cabin

Two outside rows of tall poles and a middle row of short ones support and frame this cabin. Double 2-by-10 (50 x 250mm) floor beams set in notches called daps are bolted to each row of middle poles to support the floor joists, whose ends rest on single outer floor beams; 2-by-6 (50 x 150mm) blocking nailed between the floor joists every 4 feet (1.2m) stabilizes the understructure and provides a nailing surface for plywood subflooring. Double 2-by-8 (50 x 200mm) eave beams set in daps and bolted to the outside poles support the roof framing. Stud walls sheathed with wood panels close in the walls. This roof is covered with asphalt shingles, but any roofing material described on page 98 can be laid down. A prefabricated set of steps completes the exterior of the structure.

Building the Frame to the Eaves

Putting up the poles

Dig holes for all the poles.

Cut a 2-by-10 (50 x 250mm) about 10 inches (250mm) longer than the depth of the holes.

To help guide a long outside pole into its hole, place the 2-by-10 (50 x 250mm) in the hole, then, with two helpers, brace one end of the pole against the board and tilt it up until the pole drops into the hole.

Set all the outside poles in their holes in the same way *(right)*, then lower the short middle poles into their holes.

Align all the poles and set them in concrete.

Attaching the floor beams

Start daps on the inner sides of the poles with a bucksaw, then clean out the cuts with a wood chisel.

Nail a pressure-treated 2-by-10 (50 x 250mm) floor beam in the daps in each row of poles. With a combination square, measure from the beam along both sides of each middle pole, marking a dap on the outside that will be of uniform depth and parallel to the one on the inner side.

Cut the dap, then make the remaining ones in the same way, marking all those in the row to a consistent depth *(left)*.

Nail the outer beam to the middle poles with a 3-inch (75mm) nail, then bolt all the beams in place.

Installing joists and subfloor

Cut pressure-treated 2-by-6 (50 x 150mm) joists to span across the beams, then lay them down, tying the joists to the beams with multipurpose framing anchors *(left)*. Along each side wall, nail the header joist to the ends of the floor joists in two sections, butting its inside ends against the middle pole.

Cut enough 2-by-6 (50 x 150mm) blocking to fit between adjacent joists at 4-foot (1.2m) intervals, and fasten it to the joists with 3-inch (75mm) common nails.

Nail a plywood subfloor to the joists.

Fastening the eave beams

With a helper, measure up 8 feet (2.4m) from the subfloor and mark a dap on the inner side of each pole for a double 2-by-8 (50 x 200mm) eave beam *(right)*.

Cut the daps.

Bolt the beams to the poles in the same way as you did for the floor beams.

Cut the tops of the poles flush with the upper edges of the eave beams.

Install siding, sizing the wall sections to rest flush against the middle poles. Seal the seams between the siding and poles with caulk.

Frame the roof.

A Strong Framed Roof

A basic roof frame of rafters in either shed or gable style makes an appropriate topping for a prefab frame cottage or one suspended on poles.

A Shed Roof
For this style of roof, each rafter extends over the whole width of the building. To make one side wall higher than the other, modify some of the techniques prescribed for building a basic structure. For the prefabricated frame cottage, use longer studs and two tiers of panels to build the higher wall. For the pole-supported cabin, install taller poles on the high side.

Gable Roofing
Rising from both walls to a central ridge beam, a gable roof *(page 92)* permits the use of lighter and less expensive rafter stock than a shed roof *(chart, page 90)*.

Roof Slope
Before choosing and cutting the rafters—and before deciding on the height of the taller wall of a shed roof—decide on the slope of the roof. While a roof with a gentle slope is lighter and faster to build, areas subject to heavy snowfalls may require a steep pitch *(page 99)*. Slope depends on the roofing material; metal roofs can have a gentler slope than roofs covered with asphalt shingles *(page 101)* or wood shakes *(page 102)*.

Siding
Install Z-flashing to seal the horizontal seams between siding panels of high shed-roof walls, or between the gables and walls of any cabin.

TOOLS
- Chalk line
- Hammer
- Carpenter's level
- Circular saw
- Handsaw

MATERIALS
- 1 x 2s (25 x 50mm), 1 x 4s (25 x 100mm), 1 x 6s (25 x 150mm)
- 2 x 4s (50 x 100mm), 2 x 8s (50 x 200mm)
- Rafter and joist lumber

- Plywood panels
- Exterior plywood siding (⅝" [15mm])
- Common nails (2" [50mm], 3" [75mm], 3½" [100mm])

- Galvanized box nails (2½" [65mm])
- Multipurpose framing anchors and nails
- Roof sheathing
- Roofing materials

Safety Tips

Protect your eyes with goggles when you are hammering and using power tools.

Choosing rafters

Refer to the chart at right when choosing the size of rafter stock. It provides the maximum span—the distance between the tops of the two side walls of a shed roof, or the ridge beam and one side wall of a gable roof—for five board sizes, depending on whether you space the rafters 16 or 24 inches (400 or 600mm) apart. If the cabin is in an area that experiences heavy snow, you will need larger lumber *(page 99)*.

Rafter Spacing Board Size	16" (400mm) Maximum Span	24" (600mm) Maximum Span
2 × 4 (50 x 100mm)	5' (1.5m)	N/A
2 × 6 (50 x 150mm)	9' (2.7m)	6½' (2.1m)
2 × 8 (50 x 200mm)	11' (3.3m)	9½' (3m)
2 ×10 (50 x 250mm)	14' (4.2m)	12' (3.6m)
2 × 12 (50 x 300mm)	18' (5.5m)	15½' (4.75m)

Framing a Shed Roof

Top Plate

Rafter Stock

Top Plate

Marking the bird's-mouth cuts

Snap a chalk line down the middle of a rafter board and hold the board against the end of the building so that the chalk line touches the top plates of the high and low walls.

   Tack the board to the plates.

   At the low end of the board, outline the top plate and outside of the wall *(above)*. At the high end, mark the top plate and inside of the wall.

Marking the overhang cuts

Have your helper use a carpenter's level to mark a vertical line across the rafter board 12 to 18 inches (300–450mm) from the wall or at the point you have chosen for the overhang *(right)*. Mark the same overhang at the high end of the rafter.

Cut each rafter end at the vertical lines, then cut the rafters along the plate outlines for the bird's-mouth notch.

End Rafter   Multipurpose Framing Anchor

Attaching the rafters

Mark rafter locations at 16- or 24-inch (400 or 600mm) intervals *(chart, opposite)* on the top plates of the two walls.

Set a multipurpose framing anchor on the top plate at each mark so the anchor's vertical flange is flush with the inside edge of the outline, then nail each one in place.

Fit a rafter over the marks at one end of the structure and nail it to the framing anchor. In a high-wind area, use hurricane ties.

Fasten the remaining rafters in the same way *(left)*.

Installing gable studs

In line with each stud of the gable walls, mark a location for a 2-by-4 (50 x 100mm) gable stud.

Hold a 2-by-4 (50 x 100mm) even with the first outline, with the wide face flat against the outsides of the wall and end rafter. Using a carpenter's level, mark the top plates and the bottom edges of the rafter *(right)*.

Cut the 2-by-4s (50 x 100mm) to length and toenail them to the top plate and rafter with 3½-inch (100mm) nails.

Finish the gable ends by fastening ⅝-inch (15mm) exterior plywood siding to the gable studs with 2½-inch (65mm) galvanized box nails.

Sheathe the rafters as you would for an A-frame, and lay down the roof.

End Rafter

Gable-wall Top Plate

Gable Stud

Constructing a Gable Roof

Installing joists

Mark ceiling joist locations on the side-wall top plates at the same interval you will use for the rafters.

For each pair of marks, cut a joist to span between the outer edges of the side-wall top plates.

With multipurpose framing anchors, fasten the first joist to the top plates 1½ inches (40mm) from the gable wall, locating the anchors on the inside faces of the joist.

Attach the rest of the joists in the same way, but place the anchors on the opposite side of the joists *(right)*. Fasten the last joist at the opposite gable wall in the same way as the first.

If the joists will cross over a load-bearing partition wall, you can use lumber half as long as the width of the cabin. Butt the joists end to end over the center of the wall's top plate and secure the seams with metal braces called gussets *(inset)*.

Nailing ridge-beam supports

For each gable wall, cut a 1-by-6 (25 x 150mm) the height of the roof peak as measured from the top plate of the end wall. Nail to it a pair of 1-by-2s (25 x 50mm) cut 14 inches (360mm) long, extending 7½ inches (190mm) above the top of the 1-by-6 (25 x 150mm) and spaced 1½ inches (40mm) apart, forming a ridge-beam support.

With 2-inch (50mm) common nails, fasten the supports to the insides of the end joists so the tops of the 1-by-2s (25 x 50mm) are at the height of the roof peak *(left)*.

Brace each support with a 1-by-4 (25 x 100mm) nailed to the joist.

Placing the ridge beam

Place plywood panels on the ceiling joists to create a temporary floor for working on the roof frame.

Cut a 2-by-8 (50 x 200mm) ridge beam the length of the cabin and mark the rafter positions on both sides of the ridge beam according to rafter spacing appropriate for your cabin.

With a helper, raise the ridge beam to the scaffolding and cradle it in its supports *(right)*.

Preparing the rafters

Mark the first rafter, drawing a miter cut at the ridge beam *(left)* and a bird's-mouth notch at the top plate.

Cut all the rafters to length.

Nailing the rafters

With one helper keeping the outermost rafter against the mark on the ridge beam, and a second helper holding the other end on the top plate and against the joist, fasten the rafter to the ridge beam with 3-inch (75mm) common nails *(right)*. In a high-wind area, use hurricane ties.

Have the helper at the lower end of the rafter nail the rafter to the joist.

Attach the opposite rafter in the same way, but toenail it to the ridge beam.

Repeat the procedure to install the pair of rafters at the other end of the structure.

Fasten the remaining rafters, but attach each rafter to the top plate with a multipurpose framing anchor before nailing it to the joist.

Trimming the joists

With a circular saw, trim the protruding corners of the joists flush with the top edges of the rafters, using the rafter as a guide for the saw blade *(left)*.

Remove the ridge beam supports, attach gable studs, and sheathe the gable ends as you would for a shed roof. Sheathe the rafters as for an A-frame, then lay down the roof.

Ready-Made Roof Framing

The simplest way to build a gable roof is with factory-made trusses *(box, below)*, eliminating the time-consuming job of cutting and fastening rafters. To make the work easier and safer, rent two adjustable scaffolds to position and fasten the units.

Ordering Trusses

A truss manufacturer or distributor can suggest the style of truss that is most suitable for your project.

The design you choose is dictated by load—including probable snow load—roof span, and slope. The roof slope—generally at least 4 inches (100mm) of vertical rise for every foot (300mm) of horizontal run—needs to be appropriate for the climate and the type of roofing material you will use. When ordering trusses, specify the size of the desired overhang at the eaves and the dimensions of the vent openings in the end trusses.

TOOLS
- Tape measure
- Hammer
- Circular saw
- Saber saw
- Scaffolds
- Carpenter's level

MATERIALS
- Stakes
- 1 x 6s (25 x 150mm), 2 x 4s (50 x 100mm)
- Exterior-grade plywood siding (⅝" [15mm])
- Trusses

- Common nails (2½" [65mm], 3" [75mm])
- Galvanized common nails (3½" [100mm])
- Galvanized box nails (2½" [65mm])

- Multipurpose framing anchors and nails
- Roof sheathing
- Roofing materials

A Truss for Every Purpose

Trusses are made of 2-by-4s (50 x 100mm) fastened into triangles with metal gussets. The sides of the triangle—called the top chords—take the place of rafters, while the base—or bottom chord—serves as a ceiling joist. Diagonal webs connect the top and bottom chords, transferring the weight of the roof to the walls of the structure.

The combination of diagonal and vertical webs in the Howe style of truss provides increased strength in an area with heavy snowfall. The Queen—essentially a Howe truss without vertical webs—is the most common design, while the Fink—with no center web—allows a catwalk storage space above the bottom chords. The Kingpost is the simplest of all, but as it has only a center web, it needs larger or higher-grade lumber to achieve the proper strength. A standard Kingpost is generally recommended for short and medium spans. End trusses have vertical webs to accommodate siding and a vent opening.

Erecting a Set of Trusses

Preparing the walls

Along the top plates of the front and back walls—or the eave beams of a pole-frame cabin—mark a truss location every 24 inches (600mm).

At each mark, fasten a multipurpose framing anchor.

With 3-inch (75mm) common nails spaced 24 inches (600mm) apart, fasten a 2-by-4 (50 x 100mm) nailer to the top plate of each gable wall, offsetting it 1½ inches (40mm) from the outside edge with a 2-by-4 (50 x 100mm) guide *(right)*.

Putting up temporary scabs

Nail a 2-by-4 (50 x 100mm) scab to a gable-wall stud about one-third of the way in from each corner so the board extends 4 feet (1.2m) above the nailer on the top plate *(left)*.

For a pole-frame cabin—where the roof is framed before the walls—position the scabs at the corners, and extend them from the ground to 4 feet (1.2m) above the eaves.

Raising the end trusses

Fasten ⅝-inch (15mm) exterior-plywood siding to each end truss, then cut a vent opening in the siding and frame it.

With two helpers on scaffolds, set an end truss upside down on top of the front and back walls. Wedge a 2-by-4 (50 x 100mm) into the peak of the truss and push it upright *(right)*. Position it between the nailer and scabs.

With 3½-inch (100mm) galvanized common nails, fasten the top chords to the scabs and the bottom ones to the nailer.

Install the other end truss in the same way.

Plumbing the trusses

Loosen the scabs from one of the end trusses and nail a long 2-by-4 (50 x 100mm) brace diagonally to the vent framing.

After you plumb the truss with a carpenter's level *(right)*, have a helper nail the brace to a stake in the ground.

Plumb the opposite end truss in the same way.

Brace

Bracing Board

Bracing the trusses

Cut several 1-by-6s (25 x 150mm) to brace the trusses as you install them, and mark truss locations on them.

Raise a truss and nail it to the first pair of framing anchors on the front and back walls.

With 2½-inch (65mm) common nails, fasten the end of a bracing board to the top chord of the end truss. In a high-wind area, use hurricane ties.

Nail the standard truss to the brace so the truss aligns with its location mark *(left)*. Nail a second brace across the top of the trusses on the opposite side of the ridge. Install and brace the remaining trusses in the same way.

Sheathe the trusses as you would for an A-frame. Nail braces across the tops of the bottom chords. Remove the scabs and install the roofing material *(page 98)*.

Covering the Roof

Many cabins, like most houses, are roofed with asphalt shingles, but two somewhat less common materials may be more appropriate for your cabin or cottage: metal roofing and wooden shakes.

Metal Roofing

Metal roofing is economical and fire resistant, and for areas subject to heavy snowfalls, it provides a slippery surface that sheds snow before it can build up. Metal panels can be applied to a roof with a pitch of at least 3 inches (75mm) of vertical rise for every 12 inches (300mm) of horizontal run. The metal roofing shown here can be purchased in kits, which are available at most farm-equipment and building-supply dealers. The roofing comes in a variety of colors, with panels cut to specified lengths and with specially formed trim pieces or flashings to fit at the eaves, rakes, and ridge. Use a screw gun or drill to drive the appropriate fasteners at the intervals indicated by the manufacturer.

The location of sealing strips and the correct overhang of the panels at rakes and eaves will also be indicated.

Shingles and Cedar Shakes

Available at home centers or lumberyards, asphalt shingles, wood shingles, and cedar shakes require at least a 4-in-12 slope. Shakes *(page 103)*, though expensive, provide the most rustic covering. The methods illustrated on the following pages, simplified from those prescribed for year-round homes, are suitable for vacation and weekend cottages in moderate climates. A starter course of smooth-surfaced shingles is laid along the eaves, and the rest of the roof is covered with rough hand-split shakes.

Shakes are laid on an open deck of 1-by-4s (25 x 100mm) spaced at an interval that is ½ inch (12mm) less than one-half the length of the shakes.

TOOLS
- Electric drill
- Screwdriver bit
- Tin snips
- Hammer
- Utility knife
- Shingler's hatchet

MATERIALS
- 1 x 4s (25 x 100mm)
- Common nails (2½" [65mm])
- Roofing nails (1¼" [30mm])
- Hot-dipped galvanized box nails (1½" [40mm], 2" [50mm], 3" [75mm])
- Roofing felt (15- or 30-pound [medium- or heavy-duty felt underlay)
- Metal-roofing kit
- Asphalt shingles
- Cedar shakes and shingles

Safety Tips

Goggles protect your eyes when you are driving nails. When working with metal roofing, wear work gloves to protect your hands. Put on nonslip rubber-soled shoes before you climb onto the roof.

Snow-Shedding Metal

Roofing Felt

Rake

Rake

Eave
Drip Edge

Installing the rake panels

Starting at the eaves, attach 30-pound roofing felt (heavy-duty felt underlay) with 1¼-inch (30mm) roofing nails, overlapping sheets by 6 inches (150mm).

At the eaves, attach the eave drip edge included in the roofing kit with the fasteners provided *(inset)*.

Lay a sealing strip on the eave drip edge, parallel to the eave, then place the first metal panel with its end overhanging the eave so it is square to the eave and rake *(above)*.

Attach the panel by driving the fasteners supplied through the sealing strip and into the roof. Then fasten the panel along its length, staggering screws along each side at 1- to 2-foot (300–600mm) intervals.

Continue installing panels along the rake in the same way until you reach the ridge.

Covering the rest of the roof

Lay a sealing strip parallel to the rake over the first rake panel, then place the rake drip edge over the strip and fasten it through the eave drip edge and sealing strip *(inset)*.

To install the other panels, place each one with its crimped edge overlapping the crimped edge on the adjacent panel, and with the overhang of the panels at the eaves equal to that of the first rake panel. Fasten the panels to the roof *(above)*.

If you need more than a single panel length to extend from the eave to the ridge, overlap successive pieces by 3 to 6 feet (1–2m), installing sealing strips at their ends. At the opposite rake, cut the last panels with tin snips, if necessary. Install them, then add the sealing strip and rake drip edge along the rake. Cover the other side of the roof in the same way.

Attaching the ridge cover

On each side of the ridge, lay a sealing strip parallel to the ridge, then position a ridge cover over the ridge and attach it to the roof by driving the screws through the sealing strips *(below)*.

An Asphalt-Shingle Roof

Ridge Shingle

Sheathing

Roofing Felt

Rake

Eave

First Course

Laying courses of shingles

Install roofing felt as for a metal roof, but lay 15-pound felt (medium-duty felt underlay).

For the starter course, cut the three tabs off the shingles with a utility knife and remove 6 inches (150mm) from the first shingle.

With four 1¼-inch (30mm) roofing nails per shingle, fasten the starter course so the shingles overhang the eaves and rakes by ¼ inch (6mm). In each shingle, drive four nails below the line of adhesive *(inset)*: one nail above each cutout and one nail 1 inch (25mm) from each end.

Fasten two shingles of the first course over the starter course.

For the second course, cut half a tab from the first shingle on the end that will abut the rake, nail it down, then attach the second shingle. Install two shingles in the third, fourth, and fifth courses in the same way, starting each one with a shingle cut half a tab shorter than the course below to create a stepped pattern on the roof.

Adhesive

Tab

Lay the sixth course by nailing a half-tab to the roof, then adding a full shingle. At the seventh course, repeat the pattern used for the first six courses. When you reach the rake, return to the eaves and add two-full size shingles to each course. Continue the process to cover the roof; trim the last course of shingles even with the ridge.

Finish the ridge with individual shingle tabs bent to cover both sides, starting with a tab at each end of the roof ¼ inch (6mm) beyond the rakes; working toward the middle, overlap succeeding tabs by 7 inches (180mm). Trim the top end of the last tab so at least 5 inches (125mm) of the tab it covers is exposed. Bend a half tab in two and nail it over the two tabs that overlap at the middle of the ridge.

Laying Down Shakes

Open Decking

Solid Decking

First Course (Shakes)

Starter Course (Shingles)

Laying a double starter course

For the first 3 feet (1m) up from the eave, install solid decking—1-by-4s (25 x 100mm) fastened edge to edge to the rafters with 2½-inch (65mm) common nails. Continue up to the ridge laying open decking. At the ridge, butt the last two rows of decking boards together.

Cover the solid decking with 30-pound roofing felt (heavy-duty felt overlay), securing it with 1¼-inch (30mm) roofing nails.

With 1½-inch (40mm) hot-dipped galvanized box nails, fasten a starter course of cedar shingles, overhanging the eave by 2 inches (50mm) and the rakes by 1½ inches (40mm).

Nail an 18-inch-wide (450mm) strip of roofing felt over the shingles, 10 inches (250mm) above the eave.

Driving 2-inch (50mm) box nails with a shingler's hatchet, lay the first course of shakes over the shingles, aligning the ends, but offsetting vertical joints by at least 1½ inches (40mm) *(left)*.

Laying the remaining courses

Cut a scrap shake to the length of the gap between decking boards—8½ inches (220mm) for 18-inch (450mm) shakes; 11½ inches (290mm) for 24-inch (600mm) shakes—and use it to align the bottom of each shake with that of the shake in the course below.

Lay an 18-inch (450mm) strip of roofing felt with its lower edge halfway between the top of the starter course and the bottom of the next course.

Fasten the second course of shakes with two 2-inch (50mm) box nails *(right)*.

Lay another strip of felt, then another course of shakes. Continue in this way to the ridge.

With 3-inch (75mm) box nails, cover the ridge with special two-piece ridge shakes: Start by doubling the ridge shakes at one end, then overlap the shakes as you move along the ridge to the other end so the corner joints alternate from one side of the ridge to the other *(inset)*.

Corner Joint

Making Shakes

You may want to cut your own shakes from cedar or redwood logs. To do so, saw a log into 16-inch (400mm) sections and mark lines at ¼-inch (6mm) intervals across the end of the section. Place the log on wood blocks, hold a frow—a special cutter available from specialty-tool suppliers—with its sharp edge against the top of the log, and strike the blade sharply with a wooden mallet *(right)*, severing the shake from the log. Do not try to cut through a knot; instead, remove the frow and move to the next mark on the log.

A Rustic Log Cabin

Log cabins are built with construction techniques all their own. Instead of stud or A-frame walls, logs are stacked one on top of another and notched to interlock at the corners.

Choosing the Timber
Log-cabin kits that include plans and precut logs are available, but you can save considerable expense if you obtain and prepare the logs yourself. Choose softwoods—cedar, pine, fir, or larch— that measure 8 to 12 inches (200–300mm) in diameter and taper very little from butt to tip. To calculate the number of logs you will need, divide the combined heights in inches of all the walls in your plan—including gables at the end walls—by the average diameter in inches of the logs. Add a few extra logs to your total to allow for errors.

Preparing the Logs
You can fell trees on your own property *(page 32)*; in some areas, you can log land of the National Forests or of a local lumber company after paying a "stumpage fee." You may be able to buy ready-to-use logs from a local utility or logging company.

Allow green logs to dry for at least six months. To prevent excessive cracking of the wood during the drying process, use a spud *(page 106)* to peel a 2-inch (50mm) strip along each log from two opposite sides; any cracking that occurs will be confined to these strips, and will be concealed as you build. Peel the bark from the rest of the log to help protect against insect damage. Stack the logs in two layers, spacing them about 3 inches (75mm) apart to allow for air circulation between them. Cover them with pine boughs and turn them every month or so to prevent uneven drying.

Building a Foundation
A log cabin requires a block-wall foundation with modifications: To compensate for the fact that the first course of logs on the front and back walls are higher than that of the side walls by one log diameter, the foundation at the front and back is built up by a course of cored half blocks. In addition, the anchor bolts embedded in the foundation must be long enough to penetrate the first course of logs and the sill plate.

TOOLS
- Log dogs
- Chain saw
- Lumber-cutting jig
- 2 x 4 (50 x 100mm) guide
- Hammer
- Electric drill
- Spade bit (1½" [40mm])
- Extension bit (¾" [18mm])
- Socket wrench
- Scribers
- Gouge chisel
- Mallet
- Caulking gun

MATERIALS
- Logs
- 2 x 8s (50 x 200mm)
- Exterior-grade plywood (¾" [18mm])
- Common nails (3½" [100mm])
- Ring-shank nails (2½" 65mm])
- Joist hangers and nails
- Anchor bolt washers and nuts
- Sill seal
- Polyethylene sheeting (6-mil [heavy-duty])
- Bricks

Gable Stud

Gable Log

Plate Log

Back Sill Log

Joists

Sill Plate

Anchor Bolt

Side Sill Log

Spike

Half Block

Front Sill Log

Anatomy of a log cabin

The masonry-block foundation for this cabin is identical to the one on page 48, except that the front and back walls are topped with an extra course of half blocks and the anchor bolts are longer, as explained opposite. Pressure-treated 2-by-8s (50 x 200mm) form the sill plates, and split and squared-off sill logs are attached with anchor bolts to the foundation. The side sill logs are installed first, then the front and back sill logs are notched to fit over them; 2-by-8 (50 x 200mm) floor joists supported by joist hangers run between the back and front sill logs. Logs notched at the corners form the walls, and are held in place by spikes driven 2 feet (600mm) from every corner and on both sides of door and window openings. On top of the front and back walls, plate logs with squared top and outside faces simplify the notching of rafter lumber at the roof. Cable logs are fastened to gable studs. The roof is put on last.

Safety Tips

Wear a hard hat, hearing protection, goggles or a face shield, work gloves, and steel-toed boots when operating a chain saw. Protect your eyes with goggles when chiseling notches in logs.

Laying Down the Side Sill Logs

Lumber-cutting Jig

2 × 4 Guide

Log Dog

Stripped Face

Flattening the side sill logs

Set a log on two scrap timbers with one of its stripped faces away from you and secure it with a log dog at each end.

Attach a 2-by-4 (50 x 100mm) guide as long as the log along its top with 3½-inch (100mm) common nails, positioning the guide so a chain saw will leave a 3- to 4-inch-wide (75–100mm) flat strip when it runs along the guide and log.

Bolt a commercial lumber-cutting jig to a chain saw and clamp the device to the guide at one end of the log.

Turn on the saw and run it with the jig along the log and guide (left), stopping at the opposite end.

Remove the guide, turn the log over 90 degrees, and repeat the process to flatten an adjacent side, and two adjacent sides of the other side sill log.

Time-Honored Cabin-Building Tools

The chain saw has replaced many of the tools once used in log-cabin construction, but a few traditional implements, available from specialized tool or antique dealers, remain essential. The double-handled drawknife is pulled along logs to smooth their surfaces. The cant hook, a pole with a spiked hook at one end, makes it easy to drag heavy logs short distances. The peeling spud, with its shovel-like blade, strips bark off logs. Log dogs are 3-foot (1m) iron bars with turned points at each end. The points are driven into a log and a nearby support to secure the log while you work on it. You'll need at least four dogs for building a log cabin. Instead of buying them, you may want to make your own (page 108).

Drawknife

Cant Hook

Peeling Spud

Log Dog

Anchor Bolt

Drilling the side sill logs

Transfer the anchor-bolt locations from the sill to the side sill logs as for the sill plate.

Drill a 2-inch-deep (50mm) hole into the logs at each bolt location with a ½-inch electric drill fitted with a 1½-inch (40mm) spade bit.

Extend each hole through the logs with a ¾-inch electrician's extension bit *(above)*.

Squaring Logs with a Lumber-Cutting Jig

Flattening or squaring logs with just a chain saw can be arduous work, and often results in uneven surfaces. Paired with a lumber-cutting jig, however, a saw can transform a felled tree into boards of any size in just minutes. Lightweight and easy to use, the jig has a U-shaped clamp with two bolts that attach to the chain saw guide bar. The jig is sized to hug the edges of a guide board fastened to the log and run along them as the saw cuts off one side of the log. The placement of the guide board determines the width of the cut.

Side Sill Log

Sill Plate

Anchoring the side sill logs

Position the side sill logs on their sill plates, slipping the holes over the anchor bolts.

Install the anchor bolts' washers and nuts and tighten the nuts with a socket wrench *(left)*.

Seal gaps between the sill logs and sill plates with sill seal, caulk, or water-impermeable foam gasket.

Starting 8 inches (200mm) from the end of each sill plate, mark a joist position across the sill logs every 16 inches (400mm).

With metal joist hangers, fasten joists to the sill logs at the marks.

Homemade Log Dogs

Instead of buying metal log dogs, you can make your own from 2-by-4s (50 x 100mm) cut 18 inches (450mm) long. Drill a ½-inch (12mm) pilot hole through a 2-by-4 (50 x 100mm) 2 inches (50mm) from each end and nail a 6-inch (150mm) spike through the hole. When securing a dog to a log, hammer the heads of the spikes rather than the 2-by-4s (50 x 100mm); otherwise, the spikes may be pushed up through the top of the holes.

Fitting the Front and Back Sill Logs

Marking the notches

Set the front sill log on the sill plate across the side sill logs and secure it with log dogs.

Adjust the points on a pair of scribers to one-half the log diameter. This measurement will leave the smallest practical gap between logs as you raise the walls; for a larger gap, decrease the distance between the scriber points, but avoid a gap larger than 2 inches (50mm).

Place one point on the outside of the front sill log and the other against the top of the side sill log. Keeping the points in a vertical line and in contact with both logs, follow the contours of the front sill log, scratching its profile on the side sill log *(right)*.

Repeat on the opposite sides.

Cutting the notches

Remove the log dogs, turn the front sill log over, and resecure it. With a chain saw, make a series of vertical cuts at 1-inch (25mm) intervals into the log within each notch outline, stopping just short of the scribed lines *(above, left)*.

Cut out the waste wood to the lines with a 2-inch (50mm) beveled gouge chisel and a mallet *(above, right)*.

Turn the log over and mark any high spots where the notches do not rest flush. Rotate and secure the log again, trim any high spots *(page 106)*, then reposition the log. Fit the back sill log on the opposite sill plate in the same way.

Attach 2-by-8 (50 x 200mm) joists to the sill logs with joist hangers, and install a vapor barrier and subfloor.

Raising the Walls

Unlike the precise measuring and planning involved in building walls with milled lumber, raising a log wall is a process of approximating and compensating. Choosing like-sized logs for corresponding positions in opposite walls helps keep the walls level. Use matched pairs of thick logs at the bottom of opposite walls; pair off thinner logs near the top. To compensate for the logs' natural taper, alternate the thick ends—called butts—within each wall.

Leveling the Courses

Check the level of the walls every second course—every odd-numbered course if the cabin will have an odd number—by measuring the front and back walls from the subfloor to the top of each wall at the corners of the cabin. If the measurements vary by more than 1 inch (25mm), place a log with thin or thick ends as needed, or adjust the depth of the next corner notch. A shallow notch will lift the end of a wall that is beginning to dip; a deeper notch will lower it. Deepen notches with care, however; a log notched too deeply rests along its length on the log below, and a structurally unsound gap appears at the top of the notch.

Doors and Windows

To install doors and windows made from scratch or bought prehung, you will need to cut and frame openings in the logs *(page 113)* that match the size of the doors and windows, including jambs. The special construction of the frames allows the walls to settle gradually without racking the doors and windows.

TOOLS

- Electric drill
- Spade bit (1½" [40mm])
- Extension bit (½" [12mm])
- Hammer
- Machine bolt
- Lumber-cutting jig
- 2 x 4 (50 x 100mm) guide
- Chain saw
- Drawknife
- Carpenter's level
- Wood chisel
- Mallet
- Caulking gun

MATERIALS

- 2 x 4s (50 x 100mm), 2 x 8s (50 x 200mm)
- Spikes (⅜" x 8" [10mm x 200mm])
- Washers (½" [12mm])
- Rope
- Common nails (2½" [65mm])
- Galvanized common nails (3½" [100mm])
- Doors, windows, and shims
- Insulation
- Caulk

Machine Bolt

Washer

Spike

Spiking the logs

After laying the first course of logs atop the sill logs, notching them as you did the sill logs, mark holes for spikes on the logs about 2 feet (600mm) from each corner and 1 foot (300mm) from each side of a planned window or door opening.

At each mark, drill a 1½-inch-diameter (40mm) hole at least ½ inch (12mm) deep into the log, then use a ½-inch (12mm) extension bit to extend each hole halfway through the log.

For each hole, use petroleum jelly to grease a ⅜-inch (10mm) spike long enough to reach from the bottom of the wider hole to the middle of the log in the course below. Slip a ⅜-inch (10mm) washer on the spike, then drive the spike into the hole with a hammer and a long machine bolt *(left)*. Mark the spike locations on the sides of the logs.

Drive spikes into each successive log in the same way, offsetting them from those in the course below by 4 to 6 inches (100–150mm).

Safety Tips

Goggles protect your eyes when you are hammering. Wear a hard hat, hearing protection, goggles or a face shield, work gloves, and steel-toed boots when operating a chain saw.

Rolling logs up a wall

When the walls get too high to lift the logs into place by hand, prop a pole against each end of the wall at a 45-degree angle.

Spike the poles to the ends of the top-course logs of the adjoining walls.

Tie two ropes around the top log of the wall and loop the ropes under the next log.

With a helper, pull the free ends of the ropes to roll the log up the poles *(right)*.

When the highest log that will have to be cut for a door or window opening is in position, saw a V-shaped notch into its top just inside each side of the planned opening *(inset)*. Make the notches deep enough to accommodate the chain saw's blade when the next course is laid.

Marks for Door or Window Opening

Lumber-cutting Jig

Guide Board

Squaring the plate logs

For the plate logs—those at the top of the front and back walls—choose two logs with little or no taper.

Set one plate log on a scrap timber and secure it with a log dog.

With a chain saw, guide board, and lumber-cutting jig *(page 107)*, square one side of the log *(left)*, then turn the log 90 degrees and square an adjoining face so the two surfaces form a right angle. Trim and smooth the cuts with a drawknife, as necessary.

Cut the second plate log in the same way.

Framing Doors and Windows

Nailing up guide strips

For each door or window opening, cut two 2-by-4 (50 x 100mm) guide strips 18 inches (450mm) longer than the height of the door or window unit.

With a 2½-inch (65mm) common nail, tack the top of a strip to an interior wall on each side of the planned opening at least 6 inches (150mm) above the top of the opening. Position the strips so a chain saw will cut through the center.

With a carpenter's level, plumb each strip *(right)*, then drive two more nails.

Fasten strips to the exterior wall that align with the interior strips.

Mark level lines across the interior walls for the top and bottom of each opening: For a door unit, measure up from the subfloor a distance of 5 inches (125mm) greater than the height of the unit; mark the top and bottom of window opening with lines as far apart as the height of the window unit plus 6 inches (150mm). Avoid locating the bottom of a window between two logs.

Drive a tapered shim on each side of the openings between the logs you'll be sawing.

Guide Strips

Shim

Mark for Top of Window Opening

Cutting out the opening

Attach a lumber-cutting jig to a chain saw and to the interior guide on the left side of the opening.

Starting at the notch at the top of the opening, run the chain saw along the guide and cut through the first log.

Attach the jig to the guide on the opposite side of the opening and cut through the same log. Remove the waste section and square the ends of the logs where the notches were located.

Complete the opening, cutting the logs one at a time *(left)*. Stop when you have removed the last full log, then remove the guide strips.

Chain-saw
Cut

Squaring the opening

At the top and bottom of the opening, saw a series of vertical cuts at 1-inch (25mm) intervals to the marked lines on the wall. Cut away the waste wood between the cuts with a wood chisel and mallet *(left)*.

Smooth the cut surfaces with a drawknife, making them flat for a window or prehung door or slanting slightly outward for a homemade door.

Flexible Frames

Instead of cutting slots in door and window frames to allow log walls to settle, you can cut dadoes 1 inch (25mm) deep and wide with a router or circular saw across the ends of the logs on each side of window or door openings. Then, cut matching dadoes along the sides of the frame and join the frame pieces to the logs with splines that fit the dadoes snugly. Because the frames are not fixed to the logs, they will remain square if the logs settle or shrink.

Dado

Spline

Window Frame

Slot

Framing the openings.

Build a rough 2-by-8 (50 x 200mm) frame as wide as the opening and high enough to leave 3 inches (75mm) of air space above a door frame and 2 inches (50mm) above a window frame. Join the frame together with 3½-inch (100mm) galvanized common nails *(above)*.

Position the frame in the wall opening with its inner edges flush with the interior wall. Plumb the frame and tack it to the logs.

At each log adjoining the opening, drill a series of linked holes through the side jamb with a ⁷⁄₁₆-inch (11mm) bit to form two vertical slots about 2 inches (50mm) wide.

The slots allow the logs to settle without pulling the frames down with them.

Drive an 8-inch (200mm) spike through the top of each slot *(inset)*, then remove the shims you previously drove.

Fill in the space above the opening with a compressible insulating material such as fiberglass. Outside, cover the space with trim attached to the header, but not the jamb. Caulk around the trim.

Finishing the Building

When the log walls are completed, you can turn to the job of roofing and closing in the cabin. Most of the roof framing is done with lumber rather than logs; the boards are all cut on the ground and then lifted into place. To make the above-ground work easier and safer, rent two scaffolds—one for each end of the cabin.

Framing the Roof

Begin the job by choosing a roof slope appropriate for the climate and the roofing material *(page 98)*. You can purchase boards for the framing or mill them from logs with a chain saw and a lumber-cutting jig *(page 107)*. The width of rafter lumber depends on the distance the rafters will span, as well as how far apart they are spaced. Find the correct size for your cabin using the chart on page 74, selecting boards that are long enough to create the overhang you want at the eaves.

Sealing the Gaps

After the roof is finished, fill all the gaps between the logs of the walls with foam backer rod sealed with adhesive chinking. The rod is available at building-supply stores; buy adhesive chinking through mail-order catalogs of log-cabin supplies. You can close in the cabin with a ready-made door, or you can build a rustic door that complements the log walls *(page 123)*.

TOOLS
- Scaffolds
- Circular saw
- Hammer
- Chalk line
- Sawhorses
- Crosscut saw
- Paintbrush
- Caulking gun
- Screwdriver
- Staple gun
- Chain saw

MATERIALS
- 1 x 2s (25 x 50mm),
  1 x 4s (25 x 100mm),
  1 x 6s (25 x 150mm),
  1 x 8s (25 x 200mm)
- 2 x 4s (50 x 100mm),
  2 x 6s (50 x 150mm),
  2 x 8s (50 x 200mm)
- Rafter lumber
- Tongue-and-groove boards
  (¾" x 8" [19mm x 150mm,
  the longest available])
- Exterior-grade plywood
  (¾" [18mm])
- Logs
- Common nails
  (2" [50mm], 3" [75mm])
- Galvanized common
  nails (3" [75mm])
- Galvanized box
  nails (2½" [65mm])
- Finishing nails (1" [25mm])
- Wood screws
  (2" [50mm], 3" [75mm]
  No. 8 [4mm])
- Roof sheathing
- Roofing materials
- Resin log stain
- Foam backer rod
- Adhesive chinking
- Wood glue
- Building paper
- Construction adhesive
- Strap hinges

Rafter · Ridge Beam · Flying Rafter · Round-Faced Plank · Bird's-mouth Cut · Plate Log · Sheathing · Collar Tie · Blocking

Anatomy of a log-cabin roof

The roof of this log cabin is built of rafters fastened to a 2-by-8 (50 x 200mm) ridge beam and to the plate logs on top of the walls. The rafters are mitered to fit against the ridge beam, and a notch called a bird's-mouth cut lets them sit securely on the plate logs. Blocking at the end rafters helps fortify the "flying" rafters of the roof's overhang. To counteract the outward push of the roof on the log walls, collar ties of 2-by-6s (50 x 150mm) are installed at every third rafter. Sheathing and round-faced planks, rather than whole logs, are used to build the gable walls to prevent them from settling and causing the roof to sag.

Safety Tips

Goggles protect your eyes when you are hammering or using power tools.

Anchoring the Ridge Beam

Labels: 1 × 2 Cleat · Plate Log · Ridge-beam Support · Plate Log

Building ridge-beam supports

At each gable wall, set up a scaffold inside the cabin. Metal scaffolding, available at tool rental centers, can be adjusted for work at various heights.

Build a support for each end of the ridge beam: Cut a 1-by-6 (25 x 150mm) about 2 feet (600mm) longer than the planned height of the roof peak and nail it to a pair of 1-by-2s (25 x 50mm) cut 14 inches (360mm) long, extending 7½ inches (190mm) above the top of the 1-by-6 (25 x 150mm) and spaced 1½ inches (40mm) apart.

Center the support board between the plate logs with the tops of the cleats at the planned height of the roof peak and fasten it to the inside of each gable wall with 3-inch (75mm) common nails *(above)*.

Nail a 1-by-4 (25 x 100mm) diagonally from the gable wall to each of the support boards to brace them.

Labels: Ridge Beam · Brace

Raising the ridge beam

Cut a 2-by-8 (50 x 200mm) ridge beam the length of the cabin plus the width of the desired gable overhang of 1 to 3 feet (300–900mm).

Mark the rafter positions on both sides of the ridge beam according to rafter spacing appropriate for your cabin *(page 74)*, aligning the outer marks with the gable walls.

With a helper, raise the ridge beam to the scaffolding and cradle it in its supports with the proper overhang at each end *(left)*.

Adding Rafters and Collar Ties

Marking the first rafter

Snap a chalk line down the middle of a length of rafter lumber of the appropriate size *(page 74)*.

With a helper, position the board against the ridge beam and plate log at one gable wall so the board overhangs the eave wall by the correct amount and the chalk line is level with the outside corner of the log. Position the upper end so the top edge is flush with the top of the ridge beam.

Mark the inside of the ridge beam on the board *(right)*.

Tack the board to the ridge beam, and have your helper tack it to the plate log, then outline the plate log on the rafter.

Cutting the rafters

Set the marked board on sawhorses and trim it at the ridge-beam mark with a circular saw or crosscut saw.

Make the bird's-mouth notch along the outline of the plate log with two cuts: Saw along the vertical line to the chalk line, then make the diagonal cut *(left)*, stopping at the end of the first cut.

Use the board as a template to mark and cut the remaining rafters, making one for each mark on the ridge beam, including the flying rafters that frame the overhang at each end of the cabin.

Flying
Rafter

Attaching the rafters

With two helpers—one holding a rafter on its
outline on the ridge beam, the other keeping it
aligned and in position on the plate log—fasten a flying
rafter to the beam with two 3-inch (75mm) common nails
(left). In a high-wind area, use hurricane ties.

Have a helper toenail the rafter to the plate log.

Nail a 1-by-4 (25 x 100mm) from the rafter to the gable
wall as a temporary brace.

Repeat the procedure to toenail a flying rafter to the
other side of the ridge beam, then install the flying rafters
at the opposite end of the cabin in the same way. Nail the
remaining rafters in place, temporarily bracing each one
with a 1-by-4 (25 x 100mm) nailed to the last one installed.

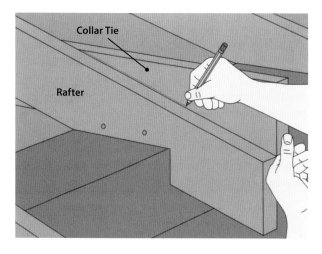

Collar Tie

Rafter

Adding the collar ties

Cut a 2-by-6 (50 x 150mm) collar tie to span between the
ends of the rafters.

With a helper, position the collar tie across the plate
logs, flat against one set of end rafters, and mark the top
edge of each rafter on the tie *(left)*.

Cut the collar tie along the marks. Use the board as a
template to mark and cut a collar tie for every third set
of rafters.

With 3-inch (75mm) common nails, fasten a collar tie to
each set of end rafters and to every third set in between.
Remove the rafter bracing and the ridge-beam supports.

Framing the Gable Ends

Framing gable ends

At equal intervals—up to a maximum of 24 inches (600mm)—along the end rafters, measure from the top edge of the rafter straight down to the top of the gable wall.

Cut a 2-by-4 (50 x 100mm) gable stud for each measurement, mitering the top end to match the roof slope. Cut a notch halfway through the stud thickness at the top end to fit behind the rafter.

With 3-inch (75mm) common nails, toenail the stud to the top of the wall. Fasten the stud to the rafter with two 2-inch (50mm) nails through the notch *(right)*.

Framing the gable overhang

Cut enough lengths of blocking from rafter lumber to fit between the end rafters and flying rafters at 16-inch (400mm) intervals.

With a helper holding the blocking in position, fasten a length to the rafters every 16 inches (400mm) with 3-inch (75mm) nails *(left)*.

Sheathe the gable ends with two layers of material. First, fasten ⁷⁄₁₆-inch (12.5mm) exterior-grade plywood to the gable studs with 2½-inch (65mm) galvanized box nails. Then cover the plywood with round-faced 2-inch-thick (50mm) planks. Miter the ends of the planks to match the roof slope, then fasten them edge to edge to the plywood with 3-inch (75mm) galvanized nails.

For the roof, lay down sheathing as for an A-frame. Then fasten any of the roofing materials described on page 98.

Sealing the Walls

Adhesive Chinking

Foam Backer Rod

Filling the gaps between logs

Clean and dry all log surfaces on both sides of the gaps between logs and between log ends and door or window frames. Brush resin log stain on the cleaned surfaces to prime them for the adhesive chinking that will fill the gaps.

Buy foam backer rod of a size that will fit snugly in the gaps, then push one length in. If necessary, drive a 1-inch (25mm) finishing nail through the rod and into a log every 4 feet (1.2m) to secure it.

Cover the rod and the remaining gaps by applying a bead of adhesive chinking *(left)*.

Building and Hanging Doors

Brace

Making the core

Trim lengths of ¾-by-8-inch (19mm x 150mm, the longest available) tongue-and-groove stock ¼ inch (6mm) shorter than the width of the door frame, cutting enough lengths to form a door at least 1½ inches (40mm) higher than its frame.

Spread wood glue on the tongues and grooves and fit the pieces together.

Cut two 1-by-8s (25 x 200mm) to the width of the door and center them along the joints at the top and bottom of the assembly. Cut a third 1-by-8 (25 x 200mm), mitering its ends to fit diagonally. With 2-inch (50mm) No. 8 (4mm) wood screws, fasten the three boards *(above)*.

Cut the door ¼ inch (6mm) shorter than its frame, trimming equally from top and bottom.

Adding a log facade

With a chain saw and a lumber-cutting jig, cut round-faced 2-inch-thick (50mm) planks from logs ¾ inch (18mm) shorter than the height of the door. Cut enough lengths to cover the face of the door.

Staple building paper to the flat face of the door.

Set the planks edge to edge on the door *(left)*, then measure how much the outside pieces extend beyond the edge.

Trimming the slabs

Holding a plank on edge between your legs, use a drawknife to trim the edge *(right)*. Remove the same amount of wood from each edge of all the planks so the outside pieces will be flush with the door edges.

Apply construction adhesive to the back of each plank, then place them on the face of the door so the bottom ends are flush with the bottom of the door. Fasten the planks with 3-inch (75mm) No. 8 (4mm) wood screws driven into the middle of each plank and spaced 6 inches (150mm) apart—or use cut nails to give the cabin a rustic appearance.

Fasten heavy-duty strap hinges to the back of the door and to the inside edge of the door frame *(left inset)*. Three hinges are recommended to hang heavy doors.

After hanging the door, position and nail 1-by-2 (25 x 50mm) doorstops on the inside of the door frame *(right inset)*.

Inside View — Strap Hinge

Outside View — Door Stops

Chapter 4
ADDING THE AMENITIES

Just because you are getting away from it all doesn't mean that you have to give up comfort, even when your cabin or cottage is not equipped with all the conveniences that you take for granted at home. Most of the basic necessities—water, heat, and waste disposal—can still be made available with a minimum of time and expense.

Tapping a Water Supply

Bringing running water to a cabin may simply involve hooking up to a public water line, but if you are off the beaten path, far from public utilities, you will need to tap a supply of surface, rain, or ground water. Before you do so, have the water analyzed by the local health department.

Aboveground Sources

Surface water from a stream or lake is the easiest to tap *(page 127)*. Rain water can be collected by means of a catchment system that runs the water to a holding tank, or cistern *(page 128)*, to be pumped out as needed. A 275-gallon (1,000-liter) cistern—a galvanized-steel pressure tank sold by plumbing suppliers—holds enough water for weekend use by a family of six.

Going Underground

Digging a well will nearly always ensure a regular water supply. At a site on sandy soil, ground water can usually be tapped easily. Check with neighbors; if their experience indicates that ground water in the area is within 30 feet (9m) of the surface, you can drive a well by hand *(page 130)*. In a soil so dense or rocky that you cannot drive a pipe, consider an old-fashioned dug well. Hire a professional to dig the shaft with a backhoe and line it with a ceramic casing. You can then install a jet pump *(page 133)* to bring up the water that collects at the bottom.

Where water is below 30 feet (9m) of the surface in any kind of soil, most people turn to a professional well driller, whose equipment can go as deep as necessary to reach water, and who can also install and seal a galvanized-steel casing. From that point, you can lower an electric pump into the well *(page 136)* and hook it up yourself.

TOOLS

- Screwdriver
- Electric drill
- Hole saw (1¾" [44mm])
- Circular saw
- Keyhole saw
- Hammer
- Tin snips
- Hand stapler
- Pipe wrenches
- Shovel
- Sledgehammer

MATERIALS

- Polyethylene pipe (1" [25mm])
- Adapters, bushings
- Hose clamps
- Plumbing-sealant tape
- Intake screen (1" [25mm])
- Concrete block
- Nylon cord
- Roof gutters and downspout
- Gutter guards
- Plastic garbage can (30-gallon [90-liter])
- Silicone sealant
- PVC adapters and bushings (1¼" [32mm], 1½" [38mm])
- PVC primer and cement
- Plywood (½" [12mm])
- 1 x 4s (25 x 100mm)
- Galvanized common nails (1½" [40mm])
- Galvanized hardware cloth (¼" [6mm] holes)
- Cistern, nipple, and vent cap
- Pump
- Galvanized steel pipe and fittings (1¼" [32mm])
- Drive point shaft
- Drive cap

An Intake for Surface Water

Assembling the pipe intake

Run 1-inch (25mm) flexible polyethylene pipe from the surface water source to the cabin.

Slide a hose clamp over the intake end of the pipe, insert a 1-inch (25mm) polyvinyl chloride (PVC) pipe adapter with male threads *(right)*, then secure the adapter by tightening the hose clamp.

Beginning at the outer end of the adapter, wrap plumbing-sealant tape around the threads, following the direction of the threads, then screw on a 1-inch (25mm) intake screen.

Adapter

Hose Clamp

Intake Screen

Positioning the pipe

Run the intake end of the pipe through the core of a concrete block.

Tie a length of nylon cord to the intake screen and place the block on the river or lake bottom as far from shore as you can safely wade. Tie the other end of the nylon cord to a float such as a stoppered plastic jug to hold the intake at least 2 feet (600mm) above the bottom *(right)*. If the bottom of the lake or river drops off immediately, go out in a rowboat, tie a long cord to the pipe, and drop the pipe and block into the water. Tie the cord to a jug.

Using an adapter, hook up the free end of the pipe to a tap if the cabin is downhill from the source. If the cabin is uphill, hook it to a pump.

Safety Tips

Protect your eyes with goggles when operating a power tool or when driving steel pipe into the ground.

A Catchment for Rainwater

Attaching gutter guards

Clean the roof gutters—or install gutters if none exist.

Add a downspout—or shorten an existing one—ending it about 3 feet (1m) above the ground.

Shield the gutter from leaves and other debris with gutter guards—5-foot (1.5m) lengths of plastic screening—cutting and bending the pieces so that they fit snugly at the sides and around the gutter's braces *(right)*.

Gutter Guard

Connecting the pipe

With a drill fitted with a 1¾-inch (44mm) hole saw, cut an opening 10 inches (250mm) from the top of a collector drum—a new 30-gallon (90-liter) plastic garbage can.

Spread silicone sealant on the threads of a 1½-inch (38mm) PVC sink-drain adapter and insert it into the hole and secure it with its nut *(left)*.

To connect the unthreaded outer end of this adapter to your plastic pipe, as shown in the inset, fasten a 1½-inch (38mm) cleanout fitting to the drain adapter with PVC cement, screw a 1½-inch-to-1¼-inch (38–32mm) reducer bushing to the cleanout fitting, and a 1¼-inch (32mm) male adapter to the reducer bushing.

Run 1-inch (25mm) flexible polyethylene pipe to the cistern and attach it to the male adapter with a hose clamp.

Drill a ⅛-inch (3mm) hole 1 to 3 inches (25–75mm) from the bottom of the drum to allow water to drain between rains to prevent stagnation.

Adapter Nut

Male Adapter   Reducer Bushing   Cleanout Fitting   Sink-drain Adapter

Assembling the elements

Place the collector drum directly under the shortened downspout.

To make a trough to break the force of the water, first cut a square of 1-inch (25mm) plywood with sides as long as the drum's outside diameter, and cut a 4-inch (100mm) hole in its center with a keyhole saw. Fasten 1-by-4s (25 x 100mm) to its sides with 1½-inch (40mm) galvanized common nails to form a box *(right)*.

With tin snips, cut a piece of galvanized hardware cloth with ¼-inch (6mm) holes to the size of the trough. Turn the box over and staple the hardware cloth to the top of the 1-by-4s (25 x 100mm).

Position the trough centered over the top of the drum.

Place a cistern as close as possible to the cabin, but downhill so its top is below the level of the outlet on the collector drum. If necessary, raise the drum on a platform or dig a pit for the cistern.

Collector Drum

Hardware Cloth

Trough Bottom

Connecting the cistern

Remove the threaded plug on top of the cistern and replace it with a nipple—a 6-inch (150mm) length of 1½-inch (38mm) pipe with male threads at each end. Screw on a 1½-inch (38mm) vent cap—a mushroom-shaped fitting with holes to let the air out of the tank as it fills.

Install a 1¼-inch (32mm) pipe adapter in the opening near the bottom of the cistern.

Slip a hose clamp over the pipe from the collector drum and push the pipe onto the adapter *(left)*. Tighten the hose clamp.

Insert a 1¼-to-1-inch (32–25mm) threaded reducer bushing into the opening near the bottom of the tank opposite the intake from the drum.

Run another length of pipe from the reducer bushing to the cabin to an indoor pump—for a cistern, a lift pump or a jet pump is suitable *(pages 132–133)*.

Vent Cap

Cistern

To Pump

Reducer Bushing

Pipe Adapter

Driving a Well

Attaching a drive-point shaft

With two pipe wrenches, fasten a coupling—a short
length of pipe with female threads at both ends—
between a 4-foot (1.2m) section of 1¼-inch (32mm)
galvanized steel pipe and a drive-point shaft—a special
section of pipe with screened openings and a sharp point
at one end *(right)*.

Screw a drive cap—a piece that covers and protects the
pipe threads—to the other end of the pipe.

Dig a starter hole 2 feet (600mm) deep at the desired
location for the well.

Push the drive point into the hole.

Coupling

Drive-point Shaft

Drive Cap

Sinking pipe sections

Drive the assembly about 1 foot (300mm) into the ground
with a sledgehammer *(left)* or with a heavy-duty steel
post pounder *(left, inset)*; if the pipe starts to angle, tap it
sideways to right it.

Retighten the coupling around the pipe and drive-
point shaft, then continue driving the assembly. When it
is almost at ground level, remove the drive cap and add
another section of pipe with a coupling as before.

Continue driving the assembly into the ground and
retightening the coupling in the same way; each time
you remove the drive cap to add a section of pipe, lower
a string with a nut attached to the end inside the pipe to
test for water. When you hear a splash, you have reached
water; drive the pipe 2 feet (600mm) deeper at this point.

Capping the well pipe

Remove the drive cap and thread a 1¼-inch (32mm) steel T-fitting with a 1-inch (25mm) side outlet to the pipe *(right)*.

Tighten the fitting with a pipe wrench and close off the top with a 1¼-inch (32mm) threaded plug.

Screw a 1-inch (25mm) plastic pipe adapter to the side outlet, clamp 1-inch (25mm) flexible polyethylene pipe to it, and run the pipe to your pump.

If the flow of water is insufficient when you use the pump, the drive point screen may be clogged. To clear it, use the pump briefly and remove the plug from the top of the T-fitting—the water will fall back down the well pipe and force sand and sediment away from the screen. Repeat this procedure until water flows freely.

T-fitting

Picking the Right Pump

Depending on the source of water and the power available, your choice of pumps ranges from an old-fashioned hand-operated lift pump to more modern electric jet and submersible models.

Hand Power

The least expensive and most easily installed pump is the lift pump *(page 132)*, available at most farm-equipment supply stores, but this type of pump works only if the water level is less than 25 feet (7.5m) lower than the pump. It consists of an iron cylinder fitted with a leather-rimmed piston, a handle to move the piston, and a pipe running from the cylinder to the water supply.

Electric Pumps

Power-operated pumps will raise water any distance. The one most often used for surface-water sources is the jet pump, which pulls the water to a pressure tank. The best power pump for deep drilled wells is the submersible type *(page 136)*, which pushes water up to the tank.

If you cannot plug into utility power at or near your building site, you will need a generator supplying 4,000 watts or more to power a jet or submersible pump.

Shutting Down for the Winter

If you do not plan to use your cabin in winter, open all of the valves and draincocks in your water system—disassembling pipes if necessary—to let water out and air into parts of the system that will be exposed to freezing temperatures.

Installing a Lift Pump

Reducer Bushing

Hose Clamp

Adapter

Mounting the pump indoors

With a keyhole saw, cut a 2-inch (50mm) hole in the counter next to your sink. Run 1-inch (25mm) flexible polyethylene pipe from the water source up through the hole.

Thread a 1¼-to-1-inch (32–25mm) reducer bushing into the 1¼-inch (32mm) fitting at the bottom of the pump, then screw on a 1-inch (25mm) male adapter.

Slide a hose clamp over the pipe, push the pipe over the adapter (left), and tighten the hose clamp. Screw the pump to the countertop.

Before you work the pump handle to draw water, pour a cup of water into the top of the pump to wet the leather seals inside.

A Jet Pump

A typical installation

In the system below, an electric pump in a sheltered part of the cabin draws water up an intake pipe, through an ejector unit near the source of surface water, and up a flexible polyethylene suction pipe. Some of the water returns to the ejector through the pressure pipe; this water squirts through a nozzle in the unit, expands in a flared tube, and creates a partial vacuum that can help suck water up to the pump from depths as great as 240 feet (75m).

At the pump, the water that is not returned to the ejector flows through an outlet pipe to a pressure tank, from which it is drawn for use in the cabin. As the tank empties, its pressure drops; when it falls to a predetermined point, a pressure switch mounted on the pump closes to run the pump until the pressure is restored. When the pump is not running, a check valve located between the intake pipe and the ejector unit closes to keep the water trapped in the system.

Pump

Pressure Tank

Suction Pipe

Pressure Pipe

Check Valve

Ejector

Intake Pipe

TOOLS

- Keyhole saw
- Screwdriver
- Cable ripper
- Wire strippers
- Wrench

MATERIALS

- Lift pump
- Flexible polyethylene pipe (¾" [18mm], 1" [25mm], 1¼" [32mm])
- Bushings
- Adapters
- Hose clamps
- Ejector unit, nipple, check valve
- Jet pump
- Pressure tank and fittings
- Drain, gate, and pressure-relief valves
- Electric cable (14-gauge [75mm flex])
- Plumbing-sealant tape

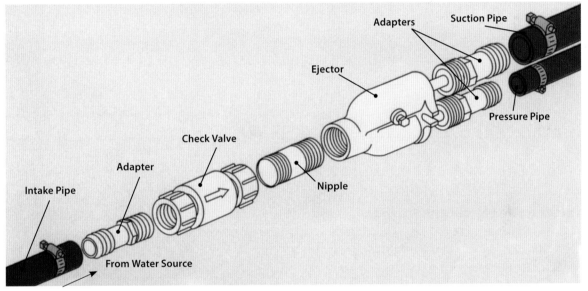

Connecting pipe to the ejector unit

Screw a nipple—a short piece of 1-inch (25mm) pipe, threaded at both ends—into the single-ended intake of the ejector, then screw the check valve onto the nipple with the valve's flow-direction arrow pointing toward the ejector.

Screw an adapter into the other end of the check valve, slide a hose clamp over the flexible polyethylene intake pipe, insert the adapter into the pipe, and tighten the hose clamp.

At the double-ended opening of the ejector, install adapters and hose clamps in the same way to hook up a 1¼-inch (32mm) suction pipe and a 1-inch (25mm) pressure pipe. (Larger pipes may be necessary for runs of more than 35 feet [10m] in length that need to raise water vertically more than 25 feet [7.5m]; consult the pump manufacturer.)

Jet Pump

Suction Pipe

To Pressure Tank

Outlet Pipe

Adapter

Pressure Pipe

To Ejector

Hooking up the pump

Join the pressure and suction pipes to the matching openings on the pump with adapters and hose clamps.

Attach ¾-inch (18mm) flexible polyethylene pipe to the pressure tank outlet with an adapter and hose clamp and run this hose to the pressure tank.

Joining the pressure-tank fittings

Begin the connections at the tank by screwing a special four-arm T-assembly, available from the pressure-tank dealer, into the threaded opening at the base of the tank.

Screw a standard T-fitting onto one side of the assembly and screw a drain valve into the top of the T-fitting.

Install a 1-inch (25mm) nipple to the other end of the T-fitting and then a gate valve, to control the flow of water to the cabin.

Screw a pressure-relief valve into the middle of the four-arm T to bleed excess pressure from the tank.

To link the tank with the jet pump, seal the two small openings at the top of the four-arm T with pipe plugs and fit the remaining opening with a 1-inch (25mm) coupling and a 1-to-¾-inch (25–18mm) reducer bushing. Connect the bushing to the pump line with an adapter and a hose clamp.

From Pump

Pressure Tank

Drain Valve

Bushing

Pipe Plugs

To Cabin

Adapter   Coupling

T-fitting

Gate Valve

Pressure-relief Valve

Four-arm T-assembly

Nipple

Line
Terminals

Clamp

From Power
Source

Ground
Wire

Ground
Screw

Wiring the pressure switch

Stretch 14-gauge (75mm flex) cable from a power source to the terminals of the pressure switch, clamp the cable to the pump, but do not hook the other end to the power source.

Screw the power wires—black and white in a 120-volt cable, black and either white or red in a 240-volt cable—to the outside switch terminals marked "Line" *(left)*. Attach the copper or green ground wire to the grounding screw. Have an electrician hook up the pump wires to the service panel or generator.

If you are working outside the U.S., check the local building regulations before doing your own electrical installations and consult a registered tradesperson if required.

Priming the pump

Open the drain valve at the pressure tank.

Remove the plug from the pump's priming port, then loosen the lock nut and tighten the stem of the water-pressure control valve *(right)*.

Pour water into the priming port until the pump is completely full, then wrap the threads of the port plug with plumbing-sealant tape and screw it loosely in place.

Turn on the pump. When air bubbles stop popping from the port, tighten the plug and loosen the valve stem until the needle on the pressure gauge is at the mark specified by the manufacturer.

Tighten the lock nut. Close the pressure tank's drain valve.

On models with a hex-head bolt to regulate the water pressure, turn the bolt according to the manufacturer's instructions to set the control valve.

Control
Valve Stem

Lock Nut

Priming Port

Pressure
Gauge

Priming
Port Plug

A Submersible Pump for a Drilled Well

Originally developed for mines and oil wells, the submersible pump has become the type most widely used in private water systems. It is silent, invisible, and virtually maintenance free.

Picking the Pieces

The professional who drills your well and installs its steel casing will recommend the size of pump you need; parts for the installation are available from pump dealers and plumbing suppliers. If your well is less than 400 feet (120m) deep, you can install the pump yourself by attaching it to flexible polyethylene pipe—ask the well driller to specify the length and grade of the pipe. Wells deeper than 400 feet (120m) require the pump to be fitted with heavy sections of galvanized-steel pipe—a job best left to the driller.

TOOLS

- Shovel
- Electric drill
- Hole saw
- Screwdriver
- Pipe wrench
- Multipurpose electrician's tool
- Wrench
- Plumbing
- Submersible pump
- Pitless adapter
- Plastic pipe
- Plastic T-fitting
- Polyethylene pipe
- Adapters
- Hose clamps
- Torque arrester

MATERIALS

- Well cap
- Pressure tank
- Check valve
- Pressure gauge
- Wiring
- Cable guards
- Electrician's tape
- Waterproof wires
- Heat-shrink splice kit
- Plastic conduit
- PVC primer and cement
- C-body
- UF cable (armored cable)
- Aluminum grounding block
- Wire caps
- Jumper wire
- Pressure switch

Pressure Tank
Junction Box
Conduit
Extension Wires
UF (Armored) Cable
Supply Pipe
Pitless Adapter
Cable Guards
Well Casing
Well Pipe
Torque Arrester
Pump

Anatomy of a submersible pump

Hung from a well pipe into the water of a drilled well, this submersible pump has a flexible torque arrester just above it that fits tightly against the well casing to keep the pipe from moving when the pump starts. The pipe itself is attached to an opening in the casing with a fitting called a pitless adapter, which seals the opening around the pipe. From this point, water flows through a supply pipe to a pressure tank.

Two waterproof extension wires and a ground wire, threaded through disks called cable guards, run up from the pump alongside the well pipe. At the top of the casing, these wires enter into an electrical junction box, where they are spliced to the wires of UF (armored) cable, designed for burial beneath the ground. The UF (armored) cable runs through a length of plastic conduit down the outside of the casing, then goes underground, in the same trench as the supply pipe, to a pressure switch mounted on the pressure tank.

Installing the System

Attaching the pitless adapter to the casing

Dig a trench to a depth just below the frost line from the house to the well casing.

Fit a drill with a steel-cutting hole saw of the same diameter as the nipple of the pitless adapter, and drill a hole into the well casing a few inches from the bottom of the trench.

Partially assemble the pitless adapter and the handle for lowering it into the casing as shown in the inset: Slip the bracket's inner gasket over the threaded nipple; leave the outer gasket, retainer, and nut for later. Make a T-shaped handle from sections of plastic pipe secured by a T-fitting and with a threaded adapter on the end. Screw the handle into the top end of the pitless adapter.

Slip the bracket onto the slider plate and lower the assembly into the casing until the nipple reaches the drilled hole.

Have a helper in the trench pull the nipple through the hole and fasten it to the casing with the outer gasket, retainer ring, and nut *(right)*.

Raise the handle, disengaging the slider plate from the bracket, and pull it out of the casing.

Handle
Slider Plate
Inner Gasket
Nipple
Outer Gasket
Nut
Retainer Ring
Bracket
Handle
Well Casing
Pitless Adapter

Well Pipe
Cable Guard

Attaching the cable guards

Slide a cable guard onto the flexible polyethylene well pipe so it is 5 feet (1.5m) from the bottom.

Wrap electrician's tape around the pipe on each side of the guard to keep it from slipping *(left)*.

Secure a guard every 15 (4.5m) feet along the pipe in the same way.

Caution

**Seal off the well hole after drilling it until you are to install the pump.
Turn power off at the source before connecting the pump wires.**

Linking the pipe and pump

Slide a pair of hose clamps onto the bottom of the well pipe and screw a flexible pipe adapter into the opening at the top of the pump *(right)*. Tighten the adapter with a pipe wrench.

Fit the pipe onto the adapter and tighten the hose clamps.

Joining the pipe and adapter

Screw a plastic adapter to the end of the pitless adapter that is opposite the handle.

Attach the well pipe to the adapter with two hose clamps *(right)*.

Temporarily seal the opening in the slider plate with tape.

Extending the pump wires

Cut a pair of submersible extension wires and a ground wire 10 feet (3m) longer than the well pipe.

Starting at the pump, run the wires along the pipe, threading them through the cable guards and leaving the extra wire at the top. Slide a length of shrink tubing—a rubber cylinder used to protect a splice—onto each pump wire, then slide a metal crimp connector over each extension wire.

Strip ½ inch (12mm) of insulation from the ends of the wires, then twist the extension wires and ground wire to the pump wires. Place the crimp connectors over the wire splices and crush the connectors *(right)*.

Slide the tubing over the splices, then heat each length with the flame from a match or lighter until it shrinks around the connector, creating a watertight seal.

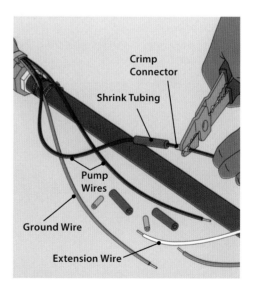

Installing the torque arrester

Loosely clamp the halves of a rubber torque arrester around the well pipe just above the pump.

Push the ends of the arrester together, expanding the middle until it matches the inside diameter of the well casing *(right)*.

Hold the arrester in position while a helper tightens the clamps.

Torque Arrester

Lowering the pump

Pad the rim of the well casing with rags to protect the pump extension wires.

Working with a helper, lower the pump into the casing *(left)*.

When the pitless adapter is near the casing, remove the tape from its slider plate and grease the rubber gasket of the plate with the lubricant supplied by the manufacturer.

With the handle, guide the plate into the bracket section of the adapter, then unscrew the handle from the adapter.

Extension Wires

Junction Box

Conduit

Well Cap

Grounding Block

Extension Wires

UF Grounding Wire

UF Wires

Assembling the conduit

With a coupling and cement, join a straight length of PVC conduit as long as the trench depth to a short curved section.

With the conduit against the well casing so the curved section is at the bottom of the trench, hold a plastic fitting called a C-body—which will serve as a junction box for the pump wiring—beside the conduit just below the top of the casing. Mark the bottom of the conduit about 1 inch (25mm) above the bottom of the junction box *(left)*, cut the conduit at the mark, and attach the junction box to it.

Run UF (armored) cable along the trench from the pressure switch, through the conduit, and into the junction box. Push the ends of the extension wires into the box.

Drill a ¼-inch (6mm) hole into the well casing near the junction box, 2 inches (50mm) from the top, then attach an aluminum grounding block to the inside of the casing with a nut and bolt.

Connections at the wellhead

Strip 8 inches (200mm) of plastic sheathing from each end of the UF (armored) cable.

At the junction box, feed the cable's bare ground wire out through the top of the box and fasten it to the setscrew of the grounding block.

With wire caps, join the cable wires to the extension wires, black to black and white to white *(left)*. Attach the extension ground wire to the grounding block setscrew.

Screw on the junction box cover and seal the well with a cap that fits over the casing and junction box, holding the box against the casing.

Pressure Gauge

Pressure Switch

From Water Source

To Cabin

Check Valve

Connecting the supply pipe

Cut a length of polyethylene pipe to run along the trench from the pitless adapter nipple to the pressure tank.

Screw an adapter to the nipple and attach the pipe to the nipple with a hose clamp.

Secure the pipe to the pressure tank *(above)* as for a jet pump, but substitute a check valve for the 1-inch (25mm) coupling, and install a pressure gauge and a pressure switch in the small openings on the T-assembly.

At the pressure switch, connect the black and white cable wires to the inside switch terminals marked "Load." Connect the wires from your power source as for a jet pump, but the leave the ground wire free. With a wire cap, join the ground wires of the power source to a short jumper wire, then connect the jumper to the switch grounding screw.

Fill the trench with earth.

Putting In an All-Purpose Sink

Even in the simplest of vacation cabins, a sink with running water is considered a basic amenity. As long as you have a supply of water—whether it is delivered by an electric pump or a hand-operated pitcher pump mounted indoors—a sink is an easily added convenience.

Choosing a Sink

The simplest sink to set up is an inexpensive plastic laundry tub, which has the added advantage of large size. However, if your pump is hand operated, you will need a surface on which to mount it; in that case, a better choice for a sink is a stainless-steel one designed to be set into a ready-made counter or a plywood shelf.

Making Connections

Flexible polyethylene pipe brings the water supply to either a pump or a faucet. Waste runs out through rigid plastic traps and T-fittings into a drain line of rigid plastic pipe leading to a drainage system.

Dealing with Waste

The waste from a sink—called gray water—generally contains such contaminants as soapsuds and food particles, so it should at least be drained to a pit *(page 147)*; but many codes require a complete septic system *(page 149)*.

TOOLS
- Screwdriver
- Pipe wrench

MATERIALS
- Plumbing-sealant tape
- Plumber's putty
- Faucet assembly
- Polyethylene pipe
- Adapter
- Hose clamp
- Sink
- Trap-and-drain assembly

Safety Tips

Wear rubber gloves when applying silicone sealant.

Faucet-hole Cover

Vent Valve

Strainer
Assembly

Tailpiece

Trap Arm

T

P Trap

Supply
Pipe

Drainpipe

A basic sink

In this installation, a standard kitchen sink is mounted in a hole cut through a ready-made counter. Water from an electric pump comes through a plastic supply pipe to a faucet attached to the middle hole of the sink; the outer holes are capped with faucet-hole covers, available from a plumbing supplier. For drainage, the sink is fitted with a strainer assembly, a tailpiece, and a P trap; from the trap,

the waste is routed to the drainpipe through a trap arm and a T-fitting. A special in-house vent valve, permissible in many areas in place of a through-the-roof vent, is attached to the top of the T.

For a hand-operated pump, the faucet is omitted and all three holes in the sink are capped. The pump is mounted on the counter so it can empty into the sink.

Preventing Leaks with Sealant

To avoid leaks at slip joints, run a bead of silicone sealant around the inside faces of all slip nuts. Spread the sealant on the threads with a finger before installing the nut and closing off joints. In the drain assembly shown above, slip joints occur between the tailpiece and strainer sleeve, the P trap and trap arm, the trap arm and trap adapter, and the trap adapter and drain pipe.

Connecting the faucet to the water supply

Wrap plumbing-sealant tape around all of the male threads of the connections between the faucet and the supply pipe.

Apply plumber's putty to the underside of the faucet base.

Fasten the faucet in the sink hole with the O-ring and nut.

Screw on the steel coupling and attach the flexible-pipe adapter to the coupling.

Mount the sink and slide the flexible polyethylene supply pipe over the adapter and secure the pipe with a hose clamp.

Faucet Base
O-ring
Nut
Coupling
Adapter
Clamp
Supply Pipe

Strainer-body Lip
Rubber Washer
Metal Washer
Vent Valve
Lock Nut
Strainer Sleeve
Slip Nut
Tailpiece
Slip Nuts
Trap Arm
Trap Adapter
P Trap
Drainpipe

Installing the drain

Apply plumber's putty to the underside of the strainer-body lip and insert the strainer body in the sink's drain hole. Slip on the rubber and metal washers and secure them with the lock nut.

Assemble the strainer sleeve, slip nut, and tailpiece and connect to the strainer body. Fasten the P trap to the tailpiece with a slip nut and washer. Connect the trap to the T with a short piece of pipe—called a trap arm. Attach a 4-inch (100mm) pipe to the top of the T, then screw on a female-threaded adapter. Coat the threads of a vent valve with petroleum jelly to ensure an airtight fit, and screw the vent into the adapter. Slip a male adapter into the bottom of the T, slide the main drainpipe over the adapter, and fasten it with a slip nut.

Attach the other end of the main drainpipe to the cabin's waste-disposal system *(page 147)*.

Self-Contained Toilets

Dealing with human waste in areas not served by traditional plumbing and sewer systems can be problematic. Septic systems are a common option *(page 149)*, but they are sometimes prohibited in areas near lakes, rivers, and water supplies, or in regions with poor soil conditions. There are two environmentally friendly waste-treatment systems that do not require a septic system *(below)*: portable chemical toilets and composting toilet systems.

Chemical Toilets
Available in several sizes, a typical unit can be used by up to six people over a three-day period.

Composting Toilets
With these units, kitchen and garden scraps can be added to the human wastes for disposal. The materials decompose and can then be recycled into the soil.

Chemical toilets
Portable chemical toilets *(above)* are made in two parts. The tank detaches from the seat for emptying. The unit is then cleaned, disinfected, and refilled with the recommended products before being reused.

Composting toilets
Composting toilets are available in two basic types. Large units *(above)* send waste into a collection tank installed outside the bathroom. These models have greater capacity than the smaller self-contained units *(above, inset)*, which collect waste in trays underneath the seat. Both types need vent pipes to release gases and evaporating liquids.

Simple and Safe Waste Disposal

Even small amounts of refuse and waste water from a cabin or cottage have to be disposed of with care—and by the method appropriate to the material. Waste involves a variety of different materials: the solid debris of day-to-day living, the liquids that drain from a sink, and die wastes from a toilet.

Solid Waste

Lower the volume of household garbage by first composting all biodegradables. Depending on local codes, the remaining waste can be burned or hauled to a dump.

Waste Water Systems

In many regions, sanitary codes forbid the practice of emptying even waste water from a wash basin onto the ground. Frequently high in phosphorus and grease, this water may contain food particles, bacteria, and viruses—substances that can pose a health hazard if they are not conducted safely away from dwelling places.

Before designing a water-disposal system, consult local health officials to determine the method required. Most sanitary codes call for a septic system *(page 149)*. In remote regions, smaller installations may be acceptable for occasional-use cabins—provided your soil can adequately absorb and filter the waste water you will generate. To test your soil, consult the U.S. Department of Agriculture extension service. If waste-water volume is fairly light and the drainage capacity of the soil is good, you may get approval to build a simple seepage pit *(page 147)* or an underground disposal bed *(page 148)*. An evapo-transpiration bed *(page 148)* may be permitted in areas of high temperature, low humidity, and poor drainage.

A Grease Trap

Any waste-water system you install must include a pretreatment tank, or grease trap, in which solids settle to the bottom and pipe-clogging greases float to the top before the water is dispersed by absorption or evaporation. Locate the trap at least 50 feet (15m) from wells or streams, and at least 10 feet (3m) from the cabin and the property line. Inspect the trap periodically, remove large accumulations of grease and solids, and dispose of them properly.

TOOLS
- Keyhole saw
- Shovel
- Mason's trowel

MATERIALS
- 30-gallon (90-liter) plastic garbage can
- PVC pipe (2" [50mm]) and fittings
- Silicone sealant
- Exterior-grade plywood (¾" [18mm])
- Geotextile fabric
- Sand
- Precast concrete distribution box
- Mortar

Safety Tips

Wear gloves and goggles when working with mortar.

Four Basic Systems

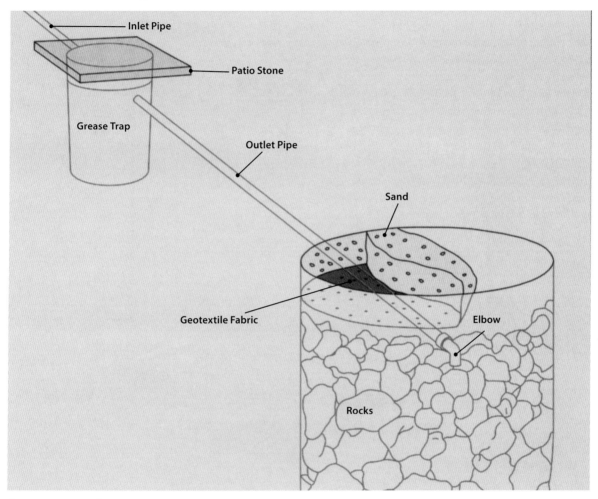

Inlet Pipe

Patio Stone

Grease Trap

Outlet Pipe

Sand

Geotextile Fabric

Elbow

Rocks

A seepage pit

In this system, waste passes from the house through an underground inlet pipe to a grease trap, which is a 30-gallon (90-liter) plastic garbage can buried up to its top. Solids will settle to the bottom of the trap, congealed greases will rise to the top, and relatively clear waste water will trickle through the outlet pipe and into the pit, slowly filtering through the pit and into the surrounding soil. The inlet pipe is 2-inch (50mm) PVC pipe attached to the cottage's wastewater outlet. The pit is dug 4 to 7 feet (1.2–2.1m) deep, 5 feet (1.5m) from the trap, and filled with irregularly shaped rocks. The outlet pipe runs underground from the trap, lies on a bed of rocks, and is covered with more rocks, geotextile fabric, and 6 inches (150mm) of sand. The trap is covered with a patio-stone lid that can be lifted off to remove and properly dispose of the built-up grease.

A network of underground pipes

Here, waste water is distributed evenly through perforated pipes to the surrounding soil. From a garbage-can grease trap *(page 150)*, the waste water flows into a concrete distribution box *(page 150)* about 5 feet (1.5m) away, where its velocity is slowed by an internal baffle or wall in the box; the water is then channeled equally to 4-inch (100mm) perforated pipes. Both the distribution box and the pipes are set level in a 3-foot-deep (1m) bed with a layer, at least 10 inches (250mm) thick, of stones ¾ to 3 inches (18–75mm) in diameter. The pipes are covered with at least 2 inches (50mm) of stones, geotextile fabric, and an 8-inch (200mm) layer of soil.

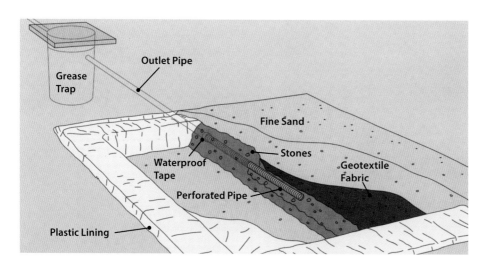

An evapo-transpiration bed

Between 1½ and 3 feet (450–900mm) deep, this bed is lined with plastic sheeting to prevent water from seeping into the soil, and filled with fine sand. Waste water runs underground from a garbage-can grease trap *(page 150)* into a 2-inch (50mm) perforated pipe that extends to the middle of the excavated bed; the pipe is surrounded by stones, covered with geotextile fabric, to prevent sand from blocking its perforations. Waterproof tape seals the area where the pipe enters the plastic liner. A bed that is used only in summer can be seeded with alfalfa to speed the evaporation process.

Labels: Septic Tank, Outlet Pipe, Soil, Geotextile Fabric, Stone

A septic tank with absorption trenches

Waste water flows from the cabin through an underground pipe to the septic tank, where solids sink to the bottom, oils and grease float to the top, and gas escapes back through the inlet pipe to the cabin drain vent. The remaining liquid, called effluent, flows slowly out into the drainage bed. The septic tank is a large watertight box made of concrete, fiberglass, or plastic that will need to be delivered by truck and installed in a pit. The sizes of the tank and drainage bed depend on the number of bedrooms in the cabin or cottage and on local requirements. The bed is typically 4 to 6 inches (100–150mm) deep. The outlet pipe from the tank is connected to a closed loop of perforated pipe with T-fittings and elbows. The pipe is laid in parallel trenches in the bed 6 to 10 feet (1.8–3m) apart, and 10 to 36 inches (250–900mm) wide, dug 1½ feet (450mm) deep. In the trenches, the pipes rest on level beds of stones at least 6 inches (150mm) thick. A layer of 2 inches (50mm) of stone and geotextile fabric is placed on the pipes, and the fabric is covered with 4 to 6 inches (100–150mm) of soil *(inset)*.

A Water-Saving Toilet

To conserve water and reduce the amount of effluence that seeps into the ground around your septic system, install a water-saving toilet. While standard flush toilets require gallons of water to push waste to a septic tank, a water-saving unit uses less than 1 quart (1 liter). Standard plastic or copper tubing supplies water to the toilet, which connects to a 3-inch (75mm) drainpipe that goes to the septic tank.

Assembling the Parts

Inlet Pipe

Elbow

Sanitary T

Extension

Making a grease trap

Cut holes into opposite sides of a 30-gallon (90-liter) plastic garbage can just below the rim. Make the holes slightly smaller than the 2-inch (50mm) PVC inlet and outlet pipes, and place the inlet hole 1 inch (25mm) higher than the outlet hole.

Dig a level pit, set the can in it, and pack soil around the can.

Dig one trench from the cabin to the inlet hole and another from the outlet hole to the drainage pit, sloping them ¼ inch per foot (5mm per 300mm).

Lay the inlet pipe in its trench and force the end into the hole in the can (above). Fill gaps around the hole with silicone sealant and attach a 90-degree elbow to the end of the pipe.

Insert and seal the outlet pipe in its hole and attach a sanitary T-fitting to the end of the pipe. To the fitting, fasten an extension that ends at least 5 inches (125mm) above the bottom of the can (inset).

Place the lid on the can, pack the remaining space around the can with soil, and conceal the container with a ¾-inch (18mm) exterior-grade plywood cover.

Connect the outlet pipe to a pit, bed, or box, then cover the inlet and outlet pipes with geotextile fabric and 6 inches (150mm) of sand.

Inlet Pipe

Outlet Pipe

Sealing a tank or distribution box

Lay all the outlet pipes at the same level and the inlet pipe at least 1 inch (25mm) higher to prevent the system from backing up—some codes require a septic-tank inlet pipe to be 3 inches (75mm) higher than the outlet pipes.

Prepare mortar from 60 percent Portland cement mix, 40 percent sand, and enough water to make the mix sufficiently stiff to stay on the joint after it is troweled on.

Fill the spaces between the pipes and the box with chips of brick and trowel on the mortar *(left)*.

Maintaining Drainage and Septic Systems

Mark off the location of the pipes and drain-field, and keep the area undisturbed. Don't drive or park cars over the system.

Practice water conservation.

Avoid pouring toxic chemicals into the drain.

If the system has a grease trap, check it periodically and remove large accumulations that have risen to the top. For a septic tank, have a professional examine it regularly—typically every two to three years—and pump it out as needed.

With any system, have it inspected if you observe any of these signs:

- Slow draining of toilets or drains.
- Sewage odors.
- Lush growth over the drainfield.
- Sewage backup in the cottage or rising to the drainfield surface after heavy rains.

Heating with Wood

Modern woodburning stoves provide an efficient way to heat a small cabin or cottage. Though it may be tempting to restore a vintage stove for a rustic cabin, a new unit is actually a wiser choice.

Selecting a Stove

Advanced-combustion or catalytic models circulate and ignite volatile gases—burning these gases accounts for more than 50 percent of the heat from a wood fire in one of these stoves. The best modern stove can heat a cabin for the winter with half the wood required by an antique type.

Stoves are made of cast iron, sheet metal, or plate steel. Cast iron is the most expensive of the three, but lasts the longest and retains heat best. A dealer can help you choose the model most suited for your cabin or cottage.

Installation

Most stoves come with enough pipe to reach an 8-foot (2.4m) ceiling; the rest of the materials are purchased separately. Buy enough pipe to meet minimum height requirements. For best results, place the stove in the middle of the cabin, but keep it at least 3 feet (1m) away from combustible materials. You can put it closer to a wall if you cover the wall with a heatproof shield; check codes on how to install the shield. Protect the floor under the stove as described opposite.

TOOLS

- Plumb bob
- Electric drill
- Utility knife
- Saber saw
- Hammer
- Putty knife
- Caulking gun
- Screwdriver
- Tin snips

MATERIALS

- Wood stove and stovepipe
- Chimney pipe, support, and cap
- Chimney pipe flashing
- Roofing cement
- Stovepipe finishing and trim collars
- Common nails (¾" [18mm])
- Roofing nails (1½" [40mm])
- Silicone caulk

Safety Tips

Wear goggles when operating a drill or driving nails; put on gloves when applying silicone caulk. Wear shoes with non-slip soles when working on the roof.

A typical installation

This stove rests on a brick hearth set on a layer of sheet metal; the hearth extends at least 1½ feet (450mm) beyond the stove on all sides. The vent system begins at the flue collar, which holds the stovepipe in place. Just below the ceiling, this uninsulated pipe meets insulated chimney pipe that supports the pipe and protects the ceiling and roof from heat. Above the roof, flashing, a storm collar, and a chimney cap keep out rain and debris, and limit downdrafts.

Chimney Pipe Support

Stovepipe

Flue Collar

Sheet Metal

Installing a Stove

Cutting the ceiling opening

With the stove in its final position, run sections of stovepipe from it to within 18 inches (450mm) of the ceiling.

Drop a plumb bob from the ceiling to the top of the pipe to mark the highest and lowest points where pipe will extend through the ceiling *(right)*, then mark the ceiling at four additional points around the perimeter of the pipe.

Remove the stovepipe sections, cover the stove with cloth or plastic, and drill a ¼-inch (6mm) pilot hole through the ceiling at each mark.

Subtract the stovepipe diameter from that of the chimney pipe, add 2 inches (50mm) for clearance, and, working on the roof, outline a circle to this distance outside the holes.

With a utility knife, cut away the roofing material and roofing felt within the circle, then cut a hole through the roof sheathing with a saber saw.

Stovepipe

Support Bracket

Installing the chimney pipe

Push the roof-support section of the chimney pipe down through the hole until the support brackets lie flat on the roof *(left)*. Nail the brackets in place with 1½-inch (40mm) roofing nails. Add one section of chimney pipe to the support.

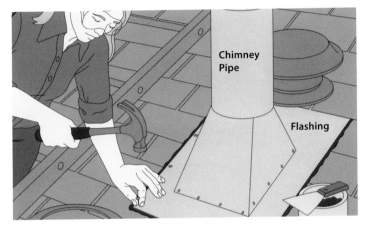

Chimney Pipe

Flashing

Installing the flashing

Fit the flashing over the chimney pipe, slipping its flanges under the shingles along the top edge, and outline it on the roof.

Remove the flashing and spread roofing cement around the outline with a putty knife.

Reposition the flashing over the pipe, press it into the roofing cement, then fasten it to the roof with 1½-inch (40mm) roofing nails *(left)*.

Add enough insulated pipe to the chimney pipe to extend the chimney 2 feet (600mm) higher than any surface within 10 feet (3m) of it.

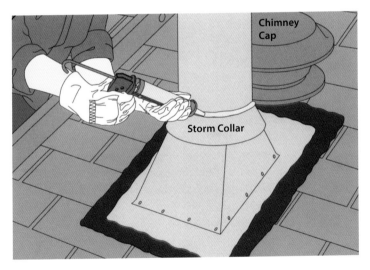

Chimney Cap

Storm Collar

Putting on the storm collar

Fasten the storm collar around the top of the flashing and seal the gap between the collar and the chimney pipe with silicone sealant from a caulking gun *(left)*.

Top the chimney pipe with a chimney cap.

Tying the pipes together

Secure the finishing collar partway down the stovepipe with setscrews, then push the top of the stovepipe up into the chimney pipe *(right)* and insert the bottom into the flue collar of the stove. If the stovepipe is too long, trim the top with tin snips.

Loosen the setscrews on the finishing collar, slide it up to the bottom of the chimney pipe, and retighten the screws.

Chimney Pipe
Support Section

Finishing
Collar

Putting on the trim collar

For easy fitting and installation, a trim collar comes in sections that resemble a necklace of aluminum rectangles, loose at their inner edges. You may need two or three sections to make a full circle around a chimney pipe.

Where the chimney pipe enters the hole in the ceiling, arrange the loose edges of a section of trim collar around the pipe and flush against the ceiling.

Fasten the collar to the ceiling with a ¾-inch common nail in every fifth grommet *(left)*.

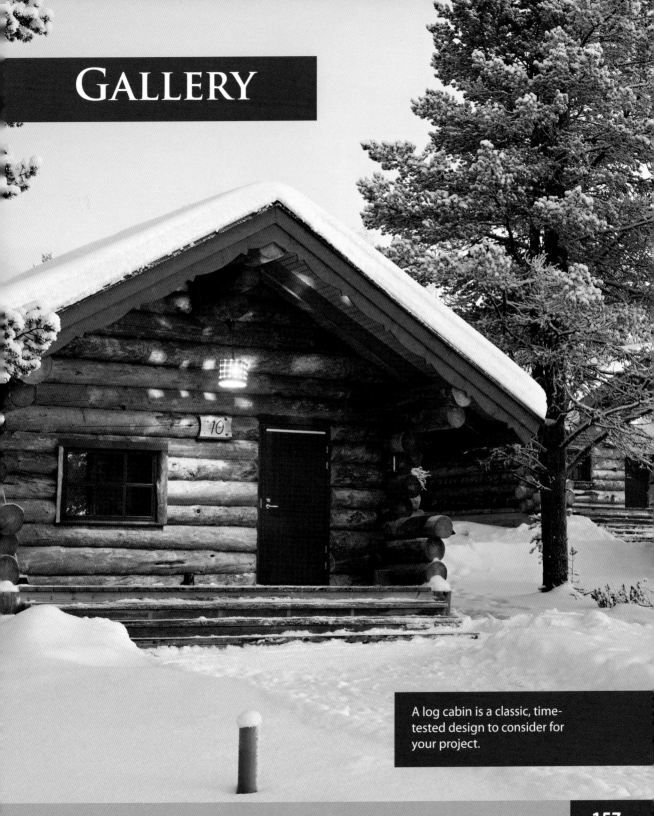

GALLERY

A log cabin is a classic, time-tested design to consider for your project.

You can make decisions about waste treatment systems based on how many people will use the cabin and how frequently—an infrequently used vacation spot will have different needs than a regular-use retreat.

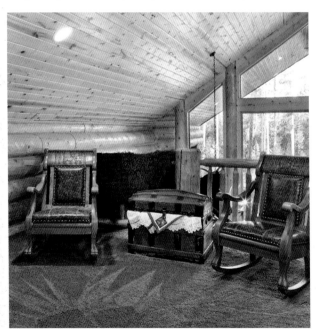

You can enjoy the natural wood of the building materials inside as well as outside your cabin.

A modern cast-iron stove effectively heats a cabin and adds a touch of charm while still being an easy-to-use, efficient utility.

Modern touches make this
A-frame cabin stand out.

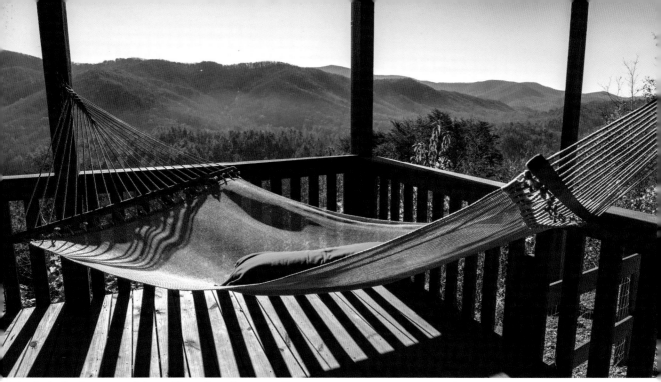

Secluded cabins are a labor of love, but they can allow you to enjoy serene, splendid views like this one.

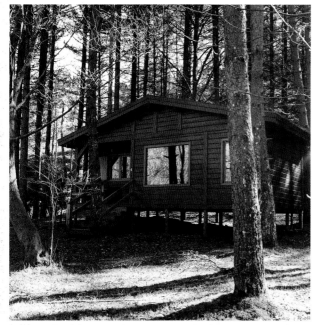

You can build your cabin up on a platform instead of directly on the ground to work with the terrain and avoid minor flooding.

Depending on the climate and weather patterns, make sure your cabin will be accessible to the road—or have whatever gear you may need to clear the path.

Depending on the exact features of the area in which you are building, a nearby natural water source can make life at your cabin much more comfortable.

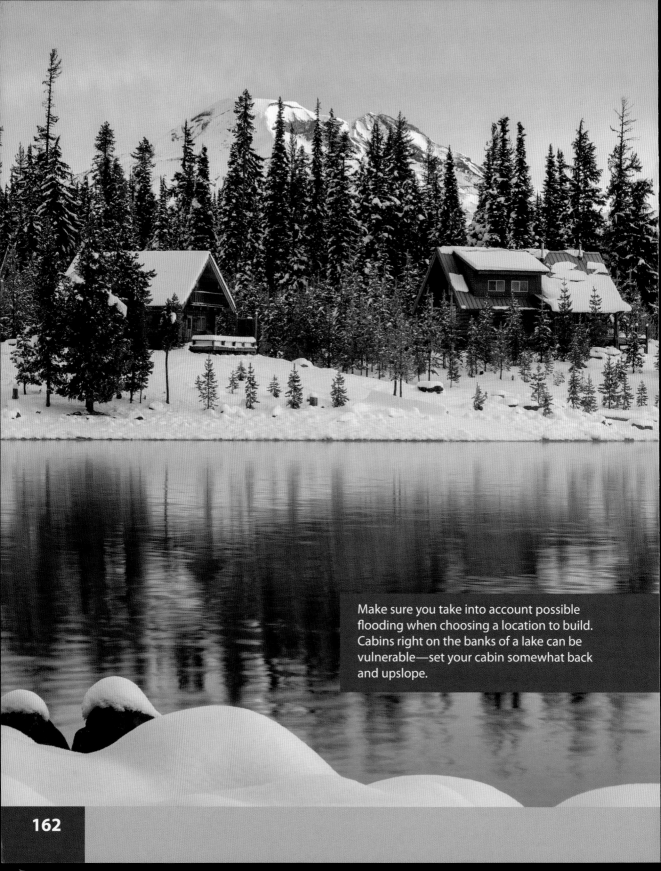

Make sure you take into account possible flooding when choosing a location to build. Cabins right on the banks of a lake can be vulnerable—set your cabin somewhat back and upslope.

There is no reason why your cabin can't have many modern amenities if it is well-designed.

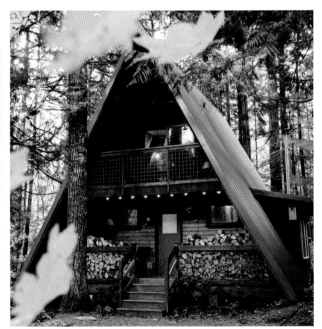

This two-level A-frame cabin is well stocked with wood for the season.

It is ideal to clear trees and brush all around the cabin to eliminate the possibility of damage from trees due to weather, earthquakes, or flooding.

You can go as modern as you want for your cabin—this small construction looks quite different from a classic log cabin.

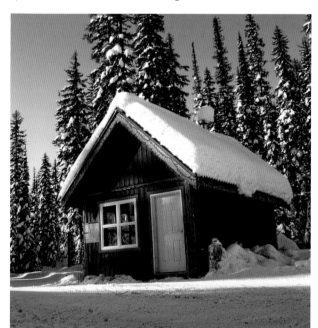

If your cabin will be in a very snowy climate, make sure you have designed a roof with the correct slope and roofing materials to accommodate it.

A cabin you build yourself can be a true reflection of your personality and provide you with the perfect retreat from the world.

INDEX

Books for Builders

Jay Shafer's DIY Book of Backyard Sheds & Tiny Houses
Build Your Own Guest Cottage, Writing Studio, Home Office, Craft Workshop, or Personal Retreat

ISBN: 978-1-56523-816-9
$19.99

The Big Book of Small Home Plans
Over 360 Home Plans Under 1200 Square Feet

ISBN: 978-1-58011-794-4
$14.99

Ultimate Guide: Barns, Sheds & Outbuildings, Updated 4th Edition
Step-by-Step Building and Design Instructions Plus Plans to Build More Than 100 Outbuildings

ISBN: 978-1-58011-799-9
$24.99

Best-Selling 1-Story Home Plans, Updated 4th Edition
Over 360 Dream-Home Plans in Full Color

ISBN: 978-1-58011-795-1
$12.99

Build Your Own Garage Manual
Over 175 Plans Inside

ISBN: 978-1-58011-789-0
$14.99

Best-Selling House Plans, Completely Updated and Revised 3rd Edition
400 Dream-Home Plans in Full Color

ISBN: 978-1-58011-761-6
$12.99

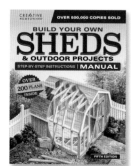

Build Your Own Sheds & Outdoor Projects Manual
Over 200 Plans Inside

ISBN: 978-1-58011-790-6
$14.99

Ultimate Book of Home Plans, Completely Updated and Revised 3rd Edition
780 Home Plans in Full Color

ISBN: 978-1-58011-721-0
$14.99

Look for These Books at Your Favorite Bookstore or Specialty Retailer
or visit www.FoxChapelPublishing.com